The Dumb
Things Sold

...just like that!

John & Kathy
CTRVD 2015
M Hamecourt

The Dumb Things Sold

...just like that!

A History of the Recreational
Vehicle Industry in America

Al Hesselbart

Library of Congress Control Number: Applied For

ISBN: 978-0-9796976-0-9

Printed in the United States of America

2nd Edition

———————————— *Dedication* ————————————

This book is dedicated to the hundreds of friends I have made through my RV experiences. Some are friends that I see only once a year at trade shows or consumer rallies. Others are friends with whom I have regular contact as a researcher and writer. It is written with thanks to the RV/MH Heritage Foundation who generously has allowed my hours of work in their library and made their extensive collection of photographs available to illustrate the stories.

— *Al Hesselbart*

l. ab
d besi
fter g
ng

Contents

Industry History

Chapter 1: Development the Recreational Vehicle Industry. 5
Chapter 2: The Evolution of the Travel Trailer. 13
Chapter 3: History of the Fifth-Wheel Hitch. .21
Chapter 4: As, Bs, Cs and Busses. 29
Chapter 5: The Growth and Development of Industry Standards 39
Chapter 6: Gypsies, Tramps, Thieves and Tin Canners 45

The Pioneers

Chapter 7: Theodore Bargman. 53
Chapter 8: Pete Callendar 57
Chapter 9: Sheldon Coleman 61
Chapter 10: Robert Crist. 65
Chapter 11: Kenneth Dixon 71
Chapter 12: Milo Miller 75
Chapter 13: Betty Orr. 81
Chapter 14: Harold Platt. 85
Chapter 15: John Schroeder 89
Chapter 16: Wilbur Schult 93
Chapter 17: Arthur Sherman. 99

The Industry Builders

Chapter 18: Wally Byam 107
Chapter 19: John Crean 111
Chapter 20: Don Boles 115
Chapter 21: Ray Frank 119
Chapter 22: John K. Hanson. 123
Chapter 23: Eugene Vesely 129
Chapter 24: Merle D. McNamee. 135
Chapter 25: Herb Reeves, Jr. 141

The rich history of the recreational vehicle industry and its related lifestyle is a story of people. It is a story of people with a dedication to a dream and people who live a dream. My book highlights the varied careers of some of the dreamers who built the industry into what it is today. From the early manufacturers who developed the concept of mobile camping vehicles, to the parts suppliers whose genius made the units more comfortable and the retailers and campground managers who brought the industry to the people, these giants in the book are among those who created today's RV lifestyle. While it is true that the RV industry grew from auto camping, RV'ers can rightfully claim roots with the pioneers who explored our nation. These were the earliest campers.

America has always been a country of dreamers. The earliest settlers came here looking for happiness and freedom to live a life of their own choosing. The early politicians promoted a drive for independence. The geniuses of the 19th and 20th centuries led our nation in an industrial revolution. These dreamers and risk-takers laid the groundwork for our nation's love of recreational travel.

When I was asked to write a series of columns on industry history for RV News(an industry trade magazine now circulated only on-line) I discovered a dynamic interest in the history of the industry. Readers, from company executives to consumer travelers, began to ask that I develop the theme into a book. After four years of research that included poring through old publications and conducting interviews with some of the subjects in the book and many other industry veterans, "The Dumb Things Sold, Just Like That" came to be. This phrase, taken from Milo Miller's poetic review of his career, seemed the most appropriate description of how our industry came into being.

Chapter 1

The Development Of The Recreational
Vehicle Industry In America

The recreational vehicle industry, popular in both America and abroad, has its roots in camping, hunting, and outdoor activities that were common long before the advent of the automobile. Travelers, including the American Plains Indians with their travois, loaded tents, provisions, cooking and sleeping equipment and pulled them around the countryside on wagons and carts long before there was any mechanical means of propulsion. Nomadic people around the world made such travel their lifestyle. American hunters camped to get provisions. American city dwellers camped for recreation. The horse-drawn gypsy caravans traveled around Central Europe more than a century before the advent of the horseless carriage. In modern time, fulltime RV'ers have lifestyles that parallel those early gypsy campers.

The advent of the automobile, in the early 1900's, greatly increased the range of travel for campers and vagabonds alike. Mechanical power made it easier for them to take more supplies and comforts along on their adventures. At first, these early "auto campers" simply piled their tents, equipment, and supplies in and on their vehicles and headed for

An early Yellowstone auto camper.

their retreats. It did not take long for the enterprising travelers to realize that carts and trailers could be attached to their cars, increasing the carrying capacity many times over. The earliest trailers were, in most cases, simply modified horse drawn carts with wooden cartwheels. But the lighter wagon wheels could not endure the bouncing caused by driving 10 to 15 miles per hour on the ruts in the dirt roads that were the early highways. Soon, the cartwheels were replaced with heavier automobile-type tires. This comfortable mode of travel, coupled with the ease in which travelers could haul and store their camping equipment, was the beginning of the modern RV lifestyle and its related industry.

By the early teens, trailers were being built not only to transport camping supplies and equipment, but to also be used as "house trailers" or mobile cabins. These earliest units were designed to store provisions, as a place to prepare and eat meals, and as a comfortable, relatively bug-proof sleeping area. "Living rooms" and most daytime activities were still relegated to the great outdoors. These first "house trailers" were usually homemade or custom built by local handymen or carriage makers. At first, no brand name companies were involved in the commercial production of camping trailers.

By the mid teens, imaginative campers were creating "house cars" by motorizing their camping vehicles. These units were primarily one-of-a-kind, custom built for personal use by the owner. Some were permanently built on auto or truck chassis. Others were exchangeable. A passenger body could be used for daily travel and then switched with a camping body for vacation travel. Early auto bodies were bolt-on structures added to a rigid frame and therefore could be removed and exchanged. Until the mid 1920's, almost all such units were homemade or one-of-a-kind, usually built by local craftsmen. Then, a few manufacturers began building multiple units for resale. The rush was on.

With the rapid growth in numbers of these early "auto campers" came a corresponding demand for safe and scenic places to camp and enjoy the out-of-doors. This need was one of the primary motivations for the development and growth of the U.S. National Park system in the early 1920's. City and county operated camping sites were becoming popular at the same time. Communities began to realize that the travelers usually brought money with them that would be spent at local businesses.

The stock market crash of 1929, and the economic disaster that followed, slowed the rise of the new industry. But the rapidly growing body of enthusiastic "trailerites", as early RV'ers were identified, wouldn't be slowed for long, even by the Great Depression. In some ways, the Depression created a new need for the mobile homes. Homeowners who lost their houses were forced into an itinerate lifestyle by economic conditions. Very shortly, the popularity of trailers was back on a meteoric

Folding tent campers first appeared in the early 1900's.

rise. By the mid 1930's, one manufacturer, The Covered Wagon Company of Mt. Clemons, Michigan, was building 40 to 50 units per eight-hour shift from a single factory. Industry production records indicate that, in 1936, one-sixth of the nation's total recorded trailer production came from that single, Detroit-area, factory.

By 1939, there were well over 100 trailer coach manufacturing companies and an even larger body of suppliers and parts distributors. Associations of manufacturers were becoming organized on both the local and national scale. These associations lobbied lawmakers and worked to promote the industry's image. Large national and international organizations of trailer owners were also springing up. Leaders in these organizations were experts at promotion who hosted popular events that were well attended by owners. Local and national retail and wholesale trailer shows were also organized, attracting large crowds. At first, all of the larger shows were held in conjunction with equally large consumer rallies and events. The Tin Can Tourists of the World, organized in 1919, had by this time become the largest of the consumer groups with hundreds of thousands of members representing both the USA and Canada. At one Tin Can Tourists rally and retail show in 1936, there were well over 1,000 units and nearly 3,000 participants in attendance.

Sergeants enforced strict rules of conduct at Tin Can Tourist camps, such as this one in Gainesville, Florida.

By 1937, a 18-foot Schult Deluxe camping trailer included many of the amenities of home.

World War II caused a second major pause in the dynamic growth of the RV industry. With strict material rationing and the conscription of many of its workers and potential customers, RV manufacturers all but halted production. Some manufacturers converted their production to various war related items. Others produced units as temporary housing for workers at war production facilities and military bases.

After the end of the war came the good times of the late 1940's and early 1950's. There was a great burst of technological advances that made trailers more comfortable. Included in this were portable propane and butane cylinders that allowed gas stoves and heaters to replace the liquid fuelled models used to date. On-board refrigeration replaced iceboxes for food preservation. Hot and cold running water was available as were on-board toilets, showers, and 110-volt generators. All of these improvements led to an increased popularity of the self-contained traveling lifestyle as a family activity.

As "baby boomers" grew up in the 1960's and began to look for inexpensive recreational activities for their young families, the RV industry experienced continued growth. Hundreds of new companies, including many of today's industry giants, sprung up across the country. The growth of what had been, up to this point, a trailer-based industry was further enhanced with the advent and availability of affordable, assembly line produced, motorhomes. The development of modern pick-up trucks also enabled the creation and popularization of the slide-in pick-up carried campers and the related "type C" motorhomes. Today these are based mostly on van chassis rather than the original pick-up truck chassis.

That 1960's boom in RV industry growth and the dramatic explosion of affordable motorized units was again nearly destroyed by economic events. The oil embargo and resultant fuel shortages and astronomically high interest rates of the 1970's, caused more than half of the manufacturers in the industry to go out of business. To survive, many merged into companies that today are giants in the industry. Through the 1970's, the lifestyle was more often referred to as camping. The rigs, whether motorized or towed, were still called "campers", just as they were fifty years earlier.

In the early 1980's, another dynamic change brought complete livability to the units. Many people, with little interest in camping and nature- based outdoor activities, became attracted to longer and larger rigs. These rigs had living room space with couches, recliners, TV, VCR, air conditioning and other home-like comforts. The lifestyle known today as RVing began to partially replace "camping" as the travel attraction. Destination oriented trips became popular, replacing the family jaunt to a favorite campsite. This alteration in comforts and conveniences made "full-timing" possible. Many retirees and some families sold their real estate based homes and resided full time on the road. Today, some RV's are better equipped with modern living accessories than the owners' permanent home. Towable rigs (travel trailers and fifth-wheel units) with prices approaching one hundred thousand dollars, not including the towing vehicle, and motorized units with high six figure and even seven digit price tags sell nearly as fast as they can be built.

From the 1930's into the early1960's, units were usually less than twenty feet long. Twelve to fifteen feet were the most common lengths. Most of the motorized, as well as the towable, units of the 1960's were less than twenty-five feet long. With improvements in both vehicles and highways, unit length grew. Thirty to forty-foot long units are common today. The added length allows the addition of more home-like features in modern RV's.

Pricing on early units varied as widely as prices do today. Entry-level towable trailers in the Depression days of the 1930's were sold in the $250 to $400 price range. Luxury trailers of that time had prices as high as $1,000. At the same time, luxury fifth wheel rigs (which were often sold with a matching tow vehicle included) and "land yacht" motorized "housecars" up to 35 feet long started at $25,000.

Today's RV lifestyle has progressed from its camping roots in the horse and buggy days, through the early auto campers, the trailerites and Tin Can Tourists of the 20's, 30's, and 40's. The medium-sized campers of the 50's and 60's were the first campers to include conveniences and comforts. But it was the upsizing of vehicles and the resulting larger units of the 70's and 80's that really allowed campers to become RV'ers and led to today's luxury RV lifestyle. This has attracted a completely new group of participants who have no real interest in camping and basic wilderness outdoor activities. The RV owner of today enjoys the many benefits of self-contained travel both as a temporary and full time lifestyle.

THE ROAD YACHT
FOR FAMILY WEEKENDS • VACATIONS • SEMI-PERMANENT LIVING

The "road yacht" touring car with living accommodations for five persons. Below: luncheon from the "galley" is spread for the auto's driver

The vehicle, which looks like a large metal bug on wheels, is the latest in touring luxury. Speed of forty-five miles an hour may be easily attained. An electric "galley," completely fitted lavatory, two sleeping cabins, book shelves, writing tables, and a radio complete the equipment of this automotive innovation, which accommodates five persons.

"Road Yacht"

$985

A Complete Home

Note compactness of bathroom unit which combines tub and shower, lavatory and roomy towel cabinet

SEE & BUY AT THE 1928 AUTO SHOWS • DEALERSHIPS ARE OPEN

Chapter 2

The Evolution Of The Travel Trailer In America

The travel trailer industry began in America around 1910. It grew out of the camping activities that were popular in our country's earliest days. In one sense, Davy Crockett, Daniel Boone and their many woodsmen brethren were simply the RV'ers of their century. With the increase in automobile ownership came a corresponding increase in auto camping. Auto camping dramatically increased the range of travel and the capacity to carry equipment over what campers could carry on foot or horseback. Early trailers were primarily homemade or custom made by local craftsmen. Very few brand name products were available until well into the 1920's. Because auto campers could carry more gear, manufacturers began to develop a wider range of camping equipment. The growth in the variety of camping equipment led builders to design bigger trailers. And thus began the first spurt of growth in the industry.

The earliest trailers were simply permanently erect canvas tents stretched over a wooden or steel pipe frame on a platform that provided a mobile bedroom with the capacity to haul other equipment. The aver-

A 1909 camping trailer.

age speed of auto travel of the period was 10 to 20 miles per hour so there was no need to collapse the tent for travel. Around 1913, some individuals began to build, or have custom-built, solid sided "tents" which provided more room and could carry permanent accessories, such as cabinetry, tables, and wardrobes. It wasn't until the later teens that kitchens began to move inside. Early campers generally cooked over wood fires. The idea of building a fire inside their small tent (solid-sided or otherwise) in order to cook took some evolution. Woodstoves were sometimes used in the larger tents of the early days but not in the personal shelters that were the small early trailers.

As the twenties approached, camping trailers were usually 8 to10 feet long to match the low towing capacity of the automobiles of the day. By miniaturizing the white gas and kerosene stoves that were commonly used in the home, they were portable enough to be used in the early campers. Coal or charcoal fuelled stoves could also be used as heating appliances. The early rigs became known as "house trailers" because the owners prepared food, ate and slept in them, not because they were originally intended for use as full time domiciles.

Canvas, plywood, leatherette, homosote, Masonite, and, in some cases, steel were used to cover trailer exteriors. Roofs were usually covered in tarpaper topped by canvas. This material could be stretched in one piece over the entire roof with no seams that would leak. The canvas was then treated with "Kool Seal", an aluminized sealer, to keep it waterproof. It was necessary to renew the sealer two or three times a year. Owners were accustomed to this type of maintenance as many of the early autos also had canvas roofs that required periodic sealing. Trailer size grew with the increase in automobile towing capacity. By the late 1920's, trailers of 15 to 20 feet in length were common and some "giants" up to 25 feet long were on the road.

The larger trailers had room for more "household" amenities. By the mid 1930's, built-in iceboxes, full white-gas kitchen ranges, sinks with running water, fuel oil furnaces, and even toilet facilities were introduced. Holding tanks for black water waste were not yet in use. The earliest toilets were either commodes over a carryout chamber pot or direct drops into a bucket or hole placed under the trailer as it was set up. Waste holding tanks and flushable toilets first appeared in the late 1930's. Interior lighting was provided by a combination of 110-volt fixtures, battery-operated lights (usually 6 volt wet cell), and gas or oil lamps. Many manufacturers provided a mixture of all three styles to fit the available service where the unit was parked. Some units were equipped with a front-mounted airplane-style propeller designed to drive a wind-powered generator to recharge the battery while underway. These were the state-of-the-art amenities until World War II.

Ralph "Red" Morgan with a 1937 Schult auto trailer.

In 1938, these folks were ready to go RV-ing in their 16-foot Schult Nomad travel trailer.

The war caused a flat spot in the rapid growth of trailer production. Rationing made many materials unavailable and manufacturers diverted most of their resources to varying kinds of defense production. Some continued building units under government contract for defense plant worker and military base housing.

Following WWII came the dramatic separation between the larger "house trailers" or mobile homes used as permanent living quarters, and campers or travel trailers used for recreation. Until this time, a trailer could be a family domicile or a portable cabin depending upon the inclination or wealth of its owner. All were small enough to be legally pulled behind a family car. In the early 1950's, combination gas/electric refrigerators began to replace iceboxes and butane or propane fuelled stoves replaced the white gas ranges for cooking in recreational units. Fuel oil heat continued as the common appliance through the 50's in those units where heat was even an available option. Air conditioning and tubs or showers for bathing were still to come. Campers simply went and jumped in the lake or stream, if one was available, to cool off and to bathe. This was the period when the term "recreational vehicle" was first coined to describe the travel trailer portion of the industry.

In the late 50's and early 1960's, pressurized water systems replaced the overhead gravity tanks or hand-operated siphon pumps, which had previously been used for fresh water storage and supply. The early gravity tanks were installed in cabinets directly over the kitchen sink. Running water was provided by gravity flow. To refill the tanks, campers generally climbed a stepladder to reach the filler cap, which was outside near the roofline of the unit. With the new pressurized systems, campers used a hand-operated air pump or the air pump at the local gas station to maintain enough air pressure to force the water through pipes into the fixtures. Dependable, on-demand, electric water pumps were still a thing of the future. Flush toilets and black water holding tanks were sometimes provided when city water and sewer hookups were available. Many campgrounds continued to provide separate toilet facilities.

Leftt: A 1950's Yellowstone camping trailer.

Below: Air conditioning is a standard feature in modern travel trailers, such as this Airstream model.

In the late 60's, the advent of one-piece molded fiberglass roofs solved many of the problems with leaking. Gasoline powered generators, previously seen only in the high-end units, showed up more often in moderately priced units. More electric appliances, including roof top air conditioners, became popular. Bathrooms with showers or tubs were available. The most common units were still "campers" and identified as such. Living room amenities were mostly unknown. The camping family prepared meals, ate, and slept in the camper but lived and interacted in the great outdoors in either rain or shine. Many campground facilities still banned the use of radios or limited their use to daytime hours. Televisions, VCRs, and telephones were the intrusions from which most campers were trying to escape. Units grew in size as towing power improved and technology reduced the weight of the travel trailers.

The 1970's were marked with economic conditions that destroyed or drove out many of the leading manufacturers. Oil shortages, lines at the gas pump, and extremely high interest rates caused consumers to delay acquiring an RV. In many cases, consumers had a hard enough time getting enough fuel just to get to and from work. The industry continued to redefine itself, even in the midst of these challenges. In the 1970's, dependable on-demand water pumps and microwave ovens were just some of the modern conveniences that led the evolution from camping to RV'ing. As household conveniences crept in, living room features began to take over much of the space.

By the 1980's, the terrible gas lines and astronomical interest rates were a thing of the past. The industry entered a new decade touting RV'ing as a popular new lifestyle. Recliner chairs, TVs, VCRs, home entertainment systems and other comforts of home filled the new campers. In these fully equipped mobile houses, families could stay cooped up inside, venturing out only when lured by absolutely perfect weather. Thousands of families who were attracted to this new outdoor lifestyle would never have considered going "camping" with its implication of roughing it outdoors amid the bugs and other critters. Suddenly, even rigs that were 35 feet long did not have enough room for everything their owners needed to be comfortable. Manufacturers began to increase the living space with two, three, and sometimes four slide-out sections.

The modern RV'ers' lifestyle is a far cry from its predecessors of

1920's and 30's. Those practitioners were outdoorsmen, hunters, and fishermen who had no modern plumbing in their homes and saw no need to clutter up their campers with such conveniences. Today's RV family enjoys the independence of being able to carry all of the comforts they desire. They go where they wish without relying on commercial transportation or public living facilities. The change in product design and function from campers to RV's has brought thousands of new customers to the industry and to the lifestyle.

Chapter 3

The History of the Fifth Wheel Hitch

The oldest general design of RV towing hitch still in use today is believed to be the fifth wheel hitch. First developed in 1917 by Glenn H. Curtiss of Curtiss-Wright aircraft fame, the towing mechanism utilizes a gooseneck trailer configuration and a vertical pin. A receiver mounted directly over the axle of the towing vehicle holds the pin. Today, the design of the hitch remains much the same as when Curtiss conceived it. His original design was created to allow larger, better-equipped trailers to be towed by early automobiles, not by trucks, as is the standard practice today.

In the Curtiss design, the receiver was mounted in the trunk or under the rumble seat of the coupes of the period. This placed the weight of the trailer directly over the rear axle as opposed to being behind the rear bumper. Early conventional travel trailers were usually connected to the tow vehicle with the type of pin or bolt hitches that were used on farm wagons and other four-wheeled trailers. Theses attached directly to the rear bumper. The ball and receiver style hitches of today had yet to be developed. In the early days, most of these pin style hitches were

The Curtiss Aerocar was designed for the well-to-do traveler.

custom fabricated for each car by local blacksmiths, as there were no manufacturers yet in existence. Weight-equalizing hitches that attached to the frame and axle of the tow vehicle had yet to be developed. Since bumper hitches were not always securely mounted to the automobile, heavy trailers were difficult to tow. The weight behind the bumper lifted the towing vehicle, resulting in a loss of control of the front wheels.

Curtiss devised a cast bracket in four segments. These were permanently mounted to the floorboards, where the car's "fifth wheel" and spare tire were originally mounted. The wheel was mounted for towing by fully deflating the tire, setting it in place inside the fixed bracket, and then re-inflating it with the air pressure holding the wheel and tire firmly in position. Hand operated tire pumps were standard equipment in early autos and trucks so this procedure required no special service or equipment. After completely removing the trunk lid or rumble seat cover from the car, the pin from the trailer gooseneck then came down into the axle hole of the wheel. Then a "C" shaped plate was bolted down to keep the pin from bouncing out of the wheel during travel on the rough and rutted dirt roads of the day. In addition to securing the trailer to the car, the inflated tire provided a degree of cushioning that Curtiss thought was necessary to protect the tow vehicle from damage or loss of control due from the jolting of the bouncing trailer.

Curtiss also designed a "motor bungalow" which he called the Curtiss Trailer. His aviation background was apparent in the technology he used in its design. Canvas and thin plywood were stretched over a wire-braced spruce frame, using a technique similar to that in the construction of aircraft of that era. The framing was, in fact, held into shape by cross wires and turnbuckles very much like early aircraft framing. This design significantly reduced the trailer's weight. Curtiss built and distributed his original motor bungalows and their accompanying fifth wheel hitch from 1917 through the early twenties.

Being somewhat of an elitist, Curtiss openly expressed his opinion that poor and working class people would spoil the activity, which he considered the special domain of the well-to do. He held this opinion despite the growth in the number of campers of moderate means. He sold the original units for extreme prices, from $1,500 to $3,500. This was at a time when the trailers of the day were either homemade or available for $150 to $500 from handyman builders. Curtiss' prices assured a large degree of exclusivity, as the average annual wage was less than $500 per year.

In 1928, recognizing the growing demand in the still infant industry, Curtiss reintroduced his motor bungalow as the Curtiss Aerocar Land Yacht. These units were completely self-contained and truly luxurious even by modern standards. Among the amenities were multiple bathrooms, servant's quarters, and Pullman type beds that folded up and out of the way when not in use. There were automotive style crank down windows throughout the land yachts. Records indicate that Curtiss obtained his window mechanisms directly from the Hudson motorcar company. The kitchens were often separated from the parlor by a wall and door as in a formal

Curtiss devised a cast bracket in four segments that was permanently mounted to the floorboard where the "fifth wheel" and spare tire were originally mounted..

house. As at home, servants usually prepared the meals. These second-generation fifth wheel units now sold for up to $25,000, definitely not for the common man. These Aerocars were still extremely lightweight for their size. Curtiss continued to use the same aircraft style, wire-braced spruce framing as in his earlier models. The exterior skin of these later units was covered with an upholstery-like padded fabric approximately one inch thick, which provided exceptional insulation. Many were outfitted with a "flying bridge" where the owners could ride in comfort and enjoy the sights while their chauffeur drove the car. In many cases, exotic custom towing vehicles were created that included living quarters for the chauffeur so that the Aerocar owners had total privacy in their unit. Curtiss produced these second-generation fifth wheel units until the beginning of World War II.

The later hitches were of the original design but downsized to hold smaller aircraft wheels and tires. This left the automobile spare tires available for use on the tow vehicle. The luxury, high-end, fifth wheel rigs quickly proved to be so popular with the traveling rich that Curtiss licensed the Detroit Aerocar Company in Detroit, Michigan to produce nearly identical rigs for mid-western consumers. His Jacksonville, Florida based production was busy meeting the needs of southeastern buyers and customers associated with Hollywood's movie business.

Fifth-wheel trailers enjoyed a rebirth in the 1960's.

A modern day fifth wheel travel trailer built by Sandpiper.

Many of the very wealthy scions of this period had private rail cars for travel. Available rails and the railroad schedules limited travel by rail. Luxury trailers gave the traveler new freedoms of destination and scheduling. Most production of RV's in the 1920's was for regional distribution. The units could only be transported by towing them to the dealer or customer one at a time on very uncertain roads. Most of the Aerocars were sold with custom appointments directly to the buyer. Some were produced for airlines or airports to use like customized limos to transport wealthy families or groups of businessmen to and from the airports. Many were built as commercial display units for sales exhibits, and not intended for use as living quarters.

Early fifth wheel RV production ended with World War II. The heavy plate and clamp receivers of modern times replaced the early hitch design, which utilized a tire. These were better suited for military transports hauling very large loads where heavy trucks were the tow vehicles. Through the war and the 1950's, the fifth wheel hitch, lost to its RV roots, was largely relegated to the military and commercial trucking industry.

The popularity of the fifth wheel rigs of today is due to a rebirth and modernization of the technology in the 1960's. Since World War II, advances were made in design and technology in the commercial trucking industry. These were downsized and adapted for the pickup trucks that had rapidly gained popularity among sportsmen and outdoor enthusiasts. These newer fifth wheel rigs were designed somewhat differently than those used the original Curtiss units and the commercial semi trailers. These new RV units were designed so that the axles were farther forward to provide a degree of balance.

This was contrary to the axles being fully at the rear of the trailer as in commercial trailers towed by heavy-duty trucks and the original Aerocars. This change in design placed more weight on the trailer axles and less on the towing vehicle, allowing for even larger trailers to be towed. Fifth wheel technology has continued to grow in popularity through the 1980's and 1990's. Huge units with multiple slide-out sections to meet the demand for more interior room are common. Because of this increase in size and space today's fifth wheel rigs are among the most luxurious of RV units available. To safely move these rigs on the highways, larger and stronger tow vehicles are now available with pulling power and braking capability approaching that of the commercial trucks.

The many full-time and serious RV'ers of today owe the concept for their 35 and 40-foot luxury fifth wheel rigs to an engineering genius who had at first competed, and then partnered with the Wright brothers in the very early days of aviation. The fifth wheel design allows operators to have living space and comfort equal to the largest motorized bus-like rigs. It gives the owners the convenience of leaving their bedroom behind by detaching the living quarters from the tow vehicle for side trips. Motorhome operators have to tow a second vehicle to get the same freedom.

Chapter 4

As, Bs, Cs and Busses
The Development of the Motorized RV

One of the earliest motorized vehicles to be factory-equipped for camping was the Touring Landau, first built by the Pierce Arrow Motor Car Company in 1910. This chauffeur-driven luxury auto included such deluxe camping appointments as a folding wash basin that attached to the back of the front seat; a holding tank for fresh water; a chamber pot-style-toilet, the predecessor to the portable potty, that fit under one side of the rear seat; and a boxed luncheon kit under the other side. Storage boxes replaced the usual running boards and the rear seat folded down into a bed.

The prices on these vehicles started at $8,250, with additional charges for accessories. This was a time in history when the common Model T Ford could be purchased for well under $1,000. While these, and other similarly convertible automobiles, were not RV's in today's sense, they were proof that the development of the RV industry was rooted in the development of the automobile.

Motorized "house cars" first appeared in the teens. They were, for the most part, homemade conversions of passenger coaches or custom bodies that replaced the passenger bodies on automobiles and early trucks. A very few early units were custom built from the ground up for the very wealthy. One of the first custom-made house cars was the Gypsy Van, a 25-foot long coach built by Conklin's Motor Bus Company. It weighed eight tons--a giant by pre-World War I standards. The Gypsy Van was powered by a six-cylinder 60 hp engine and used nine forward and three reverse gears. This behemoth made the round trip from New York to the San Francisco World Exposition in 1915, traveling almost entirely on

This 1927 motor home build by Whitfield and Sons Inc. had all electric utilities and was entirely self-contained.

The Hunt House Car was manufactured in the 1930s by cinematographer Roy Hunt.

dirt roads and wagon paths. In that era, roads were paved only around major cities.

In the 1920's, several manufacturers built "camp bodies", which were mounted on auto chassis to create house cars. A few of these were the Lamsteed Kampkar, the Wayne Touring Home, the Wiedman House Car, and the Zagelmeyer Kamper-Kar. These were usually shipped as a separate unit to the buyer, who had to mount the camper on a car or truck chassis. Some were sold, often by mail order, as a complete unit that included the chassis. The Wayne touring home featured a unique fold-down tent-covered second bed that hung off the back of the body. When alcoholic beverage production was banned in the 1920's the Anheuser-Busch Brewing Company acquired the Lamsteed Company and built Kampkar bodies during prohibition. With no dealer or distributor relationships, Anheuser-Busch sold the Kampkars by mail order through advertisements in *Field & Stream* and other outdoor magazines.

Through the 1920's and 1930's and on into the late 1940's, most motorhomes continued to be built or converted on used bus chassis. One well-known house car of the early thirties was "The Ark" built for W. K. Kellogg of corn flakes fame. Another one of these conversions, custom built in 1930 by the Pullman railroad car company, weighed more than 12 tons and pulled a Model T Ford as a "dinghy" for side trips.

Immediately after World War II, some trailer manufacturers were attracted to the idea of a house car. Many built what was truly a motorized version of their trailers. With this, the world of recreational vehicles changed, nearly overnight. The future of motorhomes was cemented when recognized manufacturers began to make them available. Still, pricing was prohibitive to most consumers. The design of post-war automobile was one factor in the demise of the camp bodies, as cars were no longer designed and built with easily removable bodies.

In 1948, the Flxible Company, a leading bus manufacturer, began a division making Land Cruiser custom coaches, house car versions of its highway coaches. This division was sold to Miles Elmers of Columbus, Ohio in 1955 and renamed Custom Coach Corporation. This company still converts bus chassis today.

In 1950, Victor Coach, a trailer manufacturer in Bristol, Indiana, began buying bare rear engine "pusher style" chassis from General Mo-

The "Victour #1" was the first motorhome off of the assembly line in 1950 at Victor Coach Company's Bristol, Indiana plant. The motor home was showcased at the Michigan State Fair.

tors to build Victour motor coaches. These units were probably the first factory produced "class A" type motorhomes with a body and interior built by an RV manufacturer on what began as a bare factory chassis. They were produced for both family and commercial use. Legendary golfer Sam Snead used a custom commercial unit to display his signature brand golf clubs for sale at the 1951 US Open golf tournament.

The largest motorhome known was produced in the early 1950's for William MacDonald of the Mid States Corporation, an early RV and mobile home manufacturer. His "Flagship" was 65 feet long and articulated so that it could bend in the middle to navigate corners. It included a foldout upper deck that doubled the width of the rear section. It also came equipped with a diving board to use with the 4-foot deep portable swimming pool that was included and which could be set up behind the unit. The upper deck could be used as a helicopter-landing pad for special promotional events. In 1953, the company offered duplicates of "The Flagship" for $100,000 each: there is no record of anyone taking them up on that offer.

The modern era of motorized RV's began in 1961 when Ray Frank bought 100 Dodge Truck chassis to make the first assembly line built house cars. Frank originally called his creation the Frank Motorhome. Later he changed the name to the Dodge Motorhome. This was the beginning of assembly line production in the industry. From this point on, "motorhome" replaced the term "house car" that had been used during the previous fifty years to describe this type of vehicle.

In the 1950's and 60's, motorhomes were popular in part because they were not affected by the 45 mph speed limits to which trailers were subjected on many highways. Through the 50's and into the early 1960's, most motorhomes were still custom made, quite expensive and targeted at an exclusive customer base. The introduction of Frank Industries Dodge Motorhome and, in the 60's, the Winnebago assembly line built coaches revolutionized the industry. The Dodge Motorhome sold through Dodge dealers for $10,900: the Winnebago was priced at $5,995. With these prices, the motorhomes became popular among working families who could previously only dream of ownership. Leaders such as Frank and Winnebago Industries' John K. Hanson proved that the public would buy their smaller "cookie cutter" vehicles. It didn't take long for sales of the production motorhome to rapidly outpace sales of the larger and much more expensive custom-made rigs that had been the industry standard for more than 30 years.

Using mass production, Winnebago was the first company to make motorhomes affordable to moderate-income families.

Other unique motorhomes of the 60's included: the Ford Condor, a near copy of the Dodge/Travco unit; the Ultra-Van built using the Chevrolet Corvair rear engine, air-cooled drive train; and the Clark Cortez, a front wheel drive model built by the Clark Equipment Company, a forklift and heavy construction equipment manufacturer. Through the latter half of the 1960's, Winnebago, Life-Time, and Beechwood made many models that retailed for under $10,000. This revolution in the industry gave motorhomes increasingly popularity among RV'ers. Between 1963 and 1973, the nation's recorded production of motorhomes exploded from approximately 200 to more than 65,000 annually.

In the late 1950's, slide-in pickup truck campers (identified as portable camp coaches) grew in popularity as an alternative to trailers or motorhomes. The manufacturers of these units developed the cab-over bed as a feature to increase available space. By the mid 1960's, as demand grew for larger and larger slide-ins, truck camper manufacturers bought pickup trucks, removed the beds and attached their larger units directly to the truck chassis. In these units, the backside of the cab was removed for easy access between the driving compartment and the camper body. Some of these early units were so long that they needed dolly wheels at the back bumper to keep the front end in contact with the road during

A modern Type C motorhome.

acceleration. Soon, chassis were extended so that the drive wheels could be placed for proper balance. In the 1970's, these chassis-mounted truck campers then evolved into chopped-off and extended van chassis, which became the "class C" motorhomes of today.

Another new product appeared in the 1960's when van campers were built from such early passenger vans as Chevrolet's Corvair-based rear engine Greenbriar, the Ford Econoline, and the Volkswagen Microbus. Ingenious owners, who saw this as a business opportunity, began to convert vans for individual owners. The popularity of these conversions led to the dynamic passenger van conversion industry of the eighties and early nineties. When the popularity of van campers grew, car manufacturers had their vans converted to sell through new car dealers. Volkswagen led this movement with its factory-converted mini-vans that were imported from Europe in the early 1960's. These miniature units grew in popularity and eventually became today's "class B" motorhomes.

Although interest in motorhoming skyrocketed during the 1960's, the industry was brought back to earth in the 1970's. Astronomical interest rates and the oil shortages of 1972-1973 and 1978-1979 drove more than half of the early motorhome manufacturers out of business. Those RV manufacturers that survived the disasters of the 1970's saw a new era in motorhomes dawn in the early 1980's.

Through the 1980's and 1990's, a steadily increasing number of comforts made motorhomes more than just camping vehicles. With generator power an expected feature, multiple air conditioners became commonplace. Living on the road full time grew in popularity. Huge basement storage compartments located beneath the coach floor gave "full timers" ample storage space. The compartments, which first appeared in the type A Fleetwood Bounders of the late 1980's and early 1990's, gave motorhome operators the luxury of storage space previously only available only to conversion coach owners.

When RV'ers began to spend more and more time on the road, demand for other creature comforts grew. Washer-dryer units began to appear as units approached 40 feet in length. Soon, longer was not enough. Newmar Corporation introduced slide outs extending the sides to add even more living area to its motorized units. At first, a living-dining space enhancement was a rarity. Then multiple slide outs began to appear, adding more bedroom and kitchen space to create a fully equipped modern apartment on wheels.

By the end of the 1990's, few observers would mistake the current motorhome for camping equipment. The 60-year-old tradition of referring to motorized RV's as campers had mostly disappeared. Motorhoming had completely come into its own as a lifestyle choice for both full and part-time practitioners who loved to travel, but did not require a wilderness destination for their trips.

The motorized RV has had a place in the automotive industry since its very earliest days. Whether the type B van unit, the temporary slide-in pickup camper, type C, type A motorhomes, or the large bus conversions, the convenience of driving your own temporary (or full time) home to the next destination feeds the American wanderlust now as it has since before the days of automobiles.

Chapter 5

The Development of Manufacturing Standards for RVs

I n the earliest days of the RV industry, there were no industry guidelines or standards for materials, design, or production techniques. Through the first three decades of industry development, from the beginning commercial production in the 1920's, through the 1940s, it was only the manufacturer's integrity that made early house cars and travel trailers safe and usable. The earliest standards applicable to the RV industry were formulated by the National Fire Protection Association. Passed in 1940, the first standards addressed fire safety concerns in trailers and trailer camps. The use of coal and white gas stoves made fire safety a major concern in the original trailers. The lack of guidelines in the infant industry created a wide discrepancy among manufacturers from those manufacturers who built the least expensive product possible to those who built the finest product without any concern for cost. Manufacturers existed at all points along this spectrum. Some products were barely serviceable and quite unsafe to use: others were built with such heavy materials that they were nearly impossible to tow.

With the many improvements in technology that came out of World

War II, each of the industry trade associations began to look for ways to standardize RV construction requirements. At this time, there were no associations that specifically represented the recreational vehicle manufacturers. The mobile home industry associations each had divisions to represent travel trailer manufacturers. The Trailer Coach Association (TCA), based in Los Angeles represented the western manufacturers. Its counterpart for the Midwest and eastern states was the Mobile Home Manufacturers Association (MHMA), based in Chicago. The travel trailer divisions in each of these associations worked with construction and appliance manufacturing associations for guidance and support in the development of enforceable standards. They considered ideas from

In the early 1950's, the TCA established a set of standards for plumbing, heating, electrical materials and construction in coaches built by their member manufacturers.

Left: *In 1969 RVI mandated that all units produced by its members must comply with A119.2.*
Right: *In the mid 1950's, six members of the Mobile Home Manufacturers Association formed the Mobile Home Craftsman's Guild and developed the Gold Seal standard of quality.*

The MHMA drafted codes that were eventually adopted the ANSI A119 standard. In 1974, when the RVI became the Recreational Vehicle Industry Association (RVIA) the ANSI A119.2 standards were modified to include fire safety.

such diverse sources as the Society of Automotive Engineers, The American Standards Association, Underwriters Laboratories, LP Gas Association, National Electrical Manufacturers Association, National Health Service, and the US Public Health Service.

In the early 1950's, the TCA established a set of standards for plumbing, heating, electrical materials and construction in coaches built by their member manufacturers. Among the criteria were inspections to be performed by an independent outside source. At first, adherence to the TCA standards was optional for its members. Those manufacturers who chose to comply were allowed to display seals on their products as evidence that they were built in compliance with the newly established codes. These TCA codes shortly became certified by the legislature as state law in California, making compliance to them mandatory for any manufacturers who marketed their products in California.

In the mid 1950's, a group of six MHMA member companies who strongly supported the establishment of mandatory standards formed the Mobile Home Craftsman's Guild. All agreed to accept these standards and display the "Gold Seal" as evidence of their adherence to the higher requirements. Gold Seal standards applied not only to heating, plumbing, and electrical components but also to chassis and axle integrity and hitch and braking capacities. As the popularity of "Gold Seal" approval grew, four additional manufacturers became members of the

Craftsman's Guild. The guild's first ten members were the largest manufacturers in the industry.

In 1958, the MHMA Board of Directors assigned Roger Reynolds, Director of the Supplier Division, the task of compiling the standards of the various groups into one set that could be enforceable nationwide. A set of committees was established to review all of the various standards applying to plumbing, electrical, and heating components and construction. Records show that over the next year, MHMA representatives sat in on more than 3600 hours of committee meetings on the subject. Association staff members and officers traveled more than 66,000 miles to attend meetings and reviews. The new standards were a result of coordination between the various political powers in MHMA, TCA, and the State of California. The final product of this massive coordinated effort was presented to the MHMA Board of Directors meeting in Mexico City in July of 1959. It was approved upon presentation. In order for the newly approved standards to achieve credibility, they needed to be approved by American National Standards Institute. After considerable negotiations, ANSI did accept the standard, assigning it ANSI number A119. This ANSI number, and its variations, still applies for RV's, Recreational Park Trailers, and Manufactured Homes.

The standards were scheduled to go into effect on March 1, 1960. Following approval of the regulations, it was necessary to develop inspection and certification procedures in order to universally enforce compliance. The inspection criteria were established and approved in time for the National Trailer Show in Louisville, Kentucky, in January of 1960. For the first time that year, all units on display had to be inspected and deemed in compliance with the new national standards.

As the RV industry separated from the mobile home industry, manufacturers realized the need for a separate trade organization. In 1963, the American Institute of Travel Trailer and Camper Manufacturers was established, in part, to represent its manufacturers and suppliers interest with policy makers. Later, that group became the Recreational Vehicle Institute (RVI). The responsibility for inspection and enforcement of ANSI A119.2 (for travel trailers and motorhomes) and ANSI A119.5 (for recreational park model trailers) fell to the new RV associations.

In 1969 RVI mandated that all units produced by its members must comply with A119.2. In 1974, RVI became the Recreational Vehicle Industry Association (RVIA), which represented the manufacturers on a national basis with continued responsibility for enforcing the ANSI standards. At the same time, the ANSI A119.2 standards were modified to also include fire safety concerns.

With the dramatic growth of the industry over the last 40 years, several regional inspection and certification engineering firms have developed and been assigned the authority to assure each manufacturers compliance with the industry-wide standards. Over the succeeding years, the standards for RV design and construction have been continuously updated and modernized to keep pace with the advances of modern technology and with new designs and inspection capabilities. Today's standards have their foundation in the efforts of early TCA, MHMA and Craftsmen's Guild members who wanted to guide their industry and assure its acceptance by their customers, the American public. The positive public opinion that the RV industry enjoys today is due, in large part, to the standard of integrity and quality set by its early leaders.

Chapter 6.

Gypsies, Tramps, Thieves, And Tin Canners: The Rise Of RV Consumer Organizations

In the winter of 1919, 22 families were camped at Desoto Auto Park, near Tampa, Florida. The park was the first public campground in the state of Florida. It continues today as Desoto State Park although not in its original location. At this point, there were very few "tourist parks" or public campgrounds available anywhere in the country. Auto campers, whether tenters or trailerites, were, for the most part, looked upon by the general public as ne'er-do wells. These early campers were commonly referred to as gypsies, trailer trash, or "tin can tourists".

However unkind were these titles, the bad reputation was in some cases earned. Some of the early campers just squatted, setting up camp wherever they wished, and leaving their trash where it lay. The tin can reference was not intended to cast dispersions on the trailers, which were often made of wood, canvas or other non-metallic materials, but referred to the campers' eating habits. The ladies of the camps did not feed their families acceptable meals of the time. To be considered a "proper" meal of the era, the food had to be prepared from scratch, either at home or in resort kitchens. The food commonly served at early campsites came from a tin can. Although this food source was necessary because of the lack of refrigeration, tin canned food was not commonly accepted, and in fact considered a poor way to feed a family.

As the members of these 22 families, these early "snowbirds", sat in a discussion around an evening campfire, James M. Morrison of Chicago suggested the formation of an organization for the benefit of all. Following extensive discussion, the Tin Can Tourists of America (TCT) was born, taking one of the insults thrown at the early campers and turning it into its new identity. They agreed to establish rules of conduct and hold regularly scheduled get-togethers. A year later, in January, 1920, the first TCT annual convention was held at Tampa.

The TCT was organized with four specific objectives: to fraternally unite all auto campers; to establish a feeling of friendship between themselves and a friendly basis with local residents; to provide clean and wholesome entertainment in camp; and to spread the gospel of cleanliness in all camps and to help enforce the rules governing public campgrounds. To these were added certain obligations including to put out

all campfires, destroy no property, to purloin nothing and help a fellow member in distress.

It was decided at the very beginning of the organization that there would be no membership fees or dues - therefore no opportunity for graft as there would be no treasury. An estimated 1200 members signed on in that first year. Each year thereafter, the volunteer leaders organized annual winter conventions in Florida and summer reunions on the shores of the Great Lakes in Ohio or Michigan. At first, there were more tenters than trailerites attending the gatherings. By 1930, most participants were using either trailers or house cars. By 1930, organization so popular that more than 1,000 rigs attended the main get-togethers. In February of 1939, almost 900 members had to camp at other sites because the primary site, which held more than 2,000 units, was full.

There is no record of how many members participated as Tin Canners in the early years, since no attempt was made to record membership until 1935. Until that time, if you attended a winter or summer meeting, took an oath to live up to the objectives and obligations and

bought a membership pin and an auto emblem, you were considered a member for life. In addition, volunteer missionary recruiters, with stocks of pins and emblems, traveled from campground to campground around the country signing up members. Members recognized each other either by the membership pins or because it became common practice to solder a tin can

The TCT reunion in 1936 in Sarasota, FL had 2626 people in attendance.

to the radiator cap of each member's car so they could be recognized in passing. Some estimate that the early organization had at least 300,000 members by 1935.

Contrary to their attitude toward campers in the early years, communities now began to compete for TCT winter conventions. An organization with thousands of campers which had its "sergeants" to enforce a strict set of rules was attractive, as was the significant amount of money they would spend in the towns along Florida's gulf coast. Meetings were held in Tampa, Sarasota, Arcadia, and Gainesville on a regular basis. Some of the Florida towns, as well as many in the Great Lakes region, actually built and operated municipal campgrounds to attract the seasonally migrating campers.

In 1937, the organization was incorporated. In recognition of the growing number of its Canadian members, the name was officially changed to The Tin Can Tourists of the World. Over the next 30 years, many efforts were made to change the name to eliminate the "tin can" slur but each failed to receive the required two-thirds majority vote from members. Following an earlier request, a list of sixteen new names was published for consideration in the July, 1938 edition of the Automobile and Trailer Travel Magazine. All of the suggested names used the same TCT initials. By the late 1930's, several other trailering groups or clubs were being formed but none was as popular or lasted as long as the TCT.

These early gatherings of RV'ers also caught the attention of the coach manufacturers. The Trailer Coach Manufacturers Association, (the first national association of trailer manufacturers) was organized following a meeting at the 1935 TCT summer reunion at Grand Rapids, Michigan. After successful regional shows in '37 and '38 the TCMA chose the 1939 summer TCT reunion near Cleveland, Ohio, as the site for the first recognized national trailer show. Large shows were held in conjunction with TCT events for many years. Today's huge Louisville, Kentucky, National RV Show is a direct descendant of that 1939 Cleveland TCMA show. The show is now open only to registered dealers: retail customers or sales are not allowed.

The annual TCT conventions and gatherings continued well into the 1980's, although the later functions were small compared to the giant gatherings of the 20's, 30's, and 40's. A great portion of the organization's remaining records and archives were assembled and are now located in the Florida State Museum in Tallahassee.

In the 1930's, the Auto Tourists Association, (ATA), was established and grew to become another major organization of trailer enthusiasts. Many other general invitation organizations (those neither brand nor model specific) have followed the pattern of the 1919 TCT creation. They came into being with the explosive growth of RV'ing in the years after World War II and include: the Family Campers and RV'ers (FCRV) (originally identified as the National Campers and Hikers Association), formed in the 1940's; the Good Sam Club (today's largest organization), founded in the 1950's; the Family Motor Coach Association (FMCA) whose membership is limited to owners of motorized RV's was formed in the 1960's; and Escapees, founded in the 1970's. All of the organizations that have followed in the path of the original Tin Can Travelers have membership rosters in the tens of thousands, with annual meetings and events attended by thousands. And all of the modern organizations more or less follow the same objectives and obligations conceived by the original TCT founders in 1919.

RV group events have become so popular that, in addition to the general membership organizations, nearly every brand name manufacturer today has a club providing events and services specifically for owners of one specific brand of RV. These clubs have many regular events and are one way for the manufacturers to attempt to develop brand loyalty in their owners. Many of these clubs have local chapters in every state of the union and local events are conducted on a monthly basis year around. Also, many clubs, founded by companies no longer in business, continue to live on with volunteer coordinators as a way for owners of such orphaned units to continue to interact and communicate with one another.

The Tin Can Tourists name has been resurrected with an organization that hosts annual antique RV gatherings each spring in Michigan and throughout the country at other times of the year. The current events are open to all but primarily feature beautifully restored vintage units. For more information on the resurrected club see www.tincantourists.com.

The Pioneers

Chapter 7

Theodore Bargman
The Development Of The OEM Supplier Industry

In 1931 a Detroit, Michigan engineer with a variety of interests in the automotive, marine and building materials industries developed an attraction to the trailer industry. He had some experience as supplier to Original Equipment Manufacturers (OEM) through his work as a parts developer and designer for aviation companies during World War I. He entered the infant trailer coach industry as a distributor for studio style couches, plumbing fixtures, and other related products. With an inventive mind, he quickly developed a wide range of new products for RV manufacturers.

By 1937, Theodore (Ted) Bargman was producing and selling his own design for door locks and hardware, sinks, and siphon style water pumps. In addition, he had developed the original combination 6 volt/110 volt interior lights as 12-volt batteries and systems were not yet in common use. He also produced electrical connectors for both 6 and 110-volt electrical systems. Through the years, he developed, manufactured, and distributed more than 40 innovative parts for the trailer industry. Among those was the plug-in wiring that connected the towing vehicle to the trailer. This continued to be an industry standard for more than 50 years. His kitchen sink for trailers had a bottom that sloped from all sides toward the drain. This improved drainage over that of the traditional level-bottomed sinks, especially when the unit could not be set up on perfectly level ground. The Bargman sink also included a novel removable strainer basket, which made for easier cleanup.

During World War II, the Bargman Company avoided the problems that occurred when material rationing restricted the parts' supplies by supplying custom-ordered machine shop and supplied parts to defense plants. He continued to provide trailer parts for the manufacturers who were building trailers for government and military housing projects. This kept him in contact with many of his trailer manufacturer customers. After the end of the war, the trailer industry rebounded when parts were once again available. To keep up with demand, the Bargman Company relocated to a new, larger facility. One of the new items Bargman developed after the war was the double basin sink. This first-of-its-kind sink became a very popular feature in trailers.

One of Bargman's oft-expressed goals was to develop a national parts distribution system. Based on the successful automobile distribution system, it would efficiently provide repair and service parts to dealers and manufacturers. With this goal in mind, he developed a system of catalogs and warehouses that made his complete line of products readily available to dealers and repair facilities from coast to coast.

From the founding of his company in 1931, until his untimely death in 1958, Ted Bargman was personally responsible for the development of most of his company's products. He would conceive a new or modified product, personally lead in its research and development, devise a workable marketing plan, then pass the project on to his management team for production and sales. When one project was done, he'd move on to his next idea. He followed this pattern for more than 25 years, during which the Bargman Company grew into the industry's primary source of parts. For the first 25 years of operation, the Bargman Company was a partnership, with Ted and his wife Mina as principals. Shortly before his death, the company incorporated as The Theodore Bargman Company.

Following his death, Ted's family and management staff continued the operation and control of the Theodore Bargman Company with Mina, serving as president until 1965. In 1968, the company opened a division in Marshall, Michigan, and later closed all of its Detroit operations in favor of the newer, larger facility. Today, the company continues its more than 70 years of service to the RV industry, as a division of the Cequent Group, a TriMas company, based out of Bloomfield Hills, Michigan.

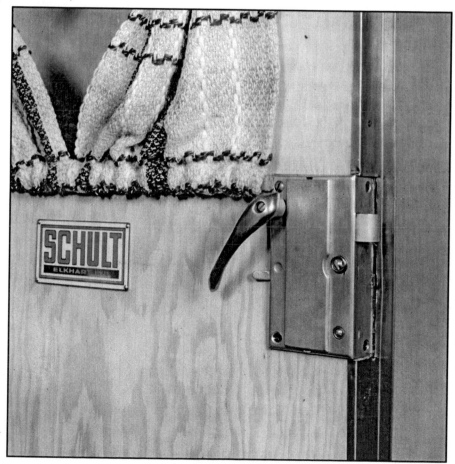

A mid-1930s Bargman door latch.

Ted Bargman was one of the early advocates for safety standards in the industry. One of his first safety accessories was the combination single taillight unit that included turn signals and a brake signal. It was centrally mounted at the rear of the trailer. Most of the very early trailers, if they had any taillight at all, displayed only a single light as a running light with no brake light/turn signal features. The hand signals drivers used for turning and braking signals weren't visible behind the trailers.

Ted Bargman, as a long time member of the Society of Automotive Engineers (SAE), was one of the key proponents for establishing and enforcing construction and safety standards for the trailer coach industry. In the mid 1950's, he arranged a meeting between industry leaders and SAE leaders to devise an enforceable set of guidelines and standards for the design and construction of trailers. The SAE leaders suggested that the American National Standards Institute (ANSI) would be a more pertinent body to certify the industry standards. In 1958, ANSI certified the original set of standards created and adopted by a team of MHMA and TCA representatives.

For his many years of dedicated service to the industry and his huge contributions to the development of trailer parts and equipment, as well as his concentration as an industry association leader on the safety and standards measures that he always promoted, Ted Bargman was posthumously inducted into the RV/MH Hall of Fame as a member of the class of 1978.

Chapter 8

Pete Callander
The Pioneer Who Just Couldn't Quit

In 1936, a 21-year-old young man chose to enhance the service offered by his filling station by creating a few parking spots for traveling "trailerites" in the area out back. Shortly thereafter, Pete Callander purchased a few units to sell and opened Southside Trailer Sales at his gas station on US 31 on the far south side of South Bend, Indiana. No other dealers existed at the time. He soon fell in love with the trailer business. Still, at the time, it was just a sideline to his service station. His early campground had 15 sites equipped with water, electricity and outhouses available. His was one of the first campgrounds in the state of Indiana to be licensed, as a tourist cabin park since no campground category yet existed for state certification. He provided the relatively uncommon luxury of full hookups.

Because of the early amenities, this campground quickly became popular with the carnival and show business people traveling to perform in the area. These show people would stay at the small campground while appearing at South Bend theaters and nightspots. In the 1930s, Pete charged them $3 per week with hookups against the $35 per week they were paid for a Thursday through Saturday show. Many of the local customers objected to his doing business with the travel trailer and show business people. They threatened to take their business elsewhere if he was going to continue doing business with these "gypsies". But Pete's clientele included many vaudeville headliners. One of his show business regulars was Fred Fontaine, who was later known for his character "Crazy Guggenheim" on the Jackie Gleason TV show. Reportedly, Pete did lose some regular gas station customers because of his trailer related customers and their business.

The early trailer exteriors were steel or Masonite: the economy units were commonly sided with oilcloth or leatherette stretched over plywood. Pete told stories of selling the early leatherette-sided trailers. He would wipe them down with olive oil diluted with gasoline to clean them and make them shine for display.

By 1950, Pete gave up his service station and put all of his efforts into trailer sales. He was instrumental in building many of the early industry associations. As one of the early presidents of the Indiana Mobile Home Association, he served two terms in 1954 and 1966, subsequently serving on that board of directors for more than 50 years. He was one of the first presidents of the national dealers association and served for twenty years on its board of directors. Pete was on the original committee to approve the ANSI 119.1 standards, which continue in use today. Until the mid 1950's, Midwest dealers attended shows in New Orleans, New York, and sometimes in Chicago. He was very involved in the establishment of the MMHA show in Louisville from which the current Louisville National RV Show evolved. He told of visiting the Kentucky Exhibition Center while it was under construction. At that time, the show was held in New York, and was very expensive for both manufacturers and dealer attendees. He told the story that the Kentucky State

Fair hosts originally charged, for the full five-day week, what the New York center charged for each day. He was also very instrumental in the development of the Midwest Show in Elkhart, Indiana, which became the current retail show in South Bend. He was the chairman for that first Midwest show in 1954. That show was created to provide exposure for the many smaller midwestern manufacturers who were not members of the large regional and national associations and thus were not invited to the early association sponsored shows. That show grew beyond the organizers' wildest dreams to become one of the nation's largest. Because of his vast experience and lifetime of commitment to the industry, Pete was selected on many occasions to represent the nation's dealers before congressional hearings in Washington, DC.

He served for many years on the Board of Directors of the RV/MH Heritage Foundation, serving as Chairman in 1993. He was also involved for many years as the leader of the foundation sponsored industry "Creators Society", an organization where industry veterans and retirees could share their experiences.

Quality service to his customers was a vital part of Pete's way of doing business. In the 1950's, Pete was one of the founders and promoters of the MDNA dealers association national service schools. He served on the service school committee and faculty for many years.

During his career, he had to relocate his business twice to find room and to accommodate zoning changes in the growing city of South Bend. Each time he moved about 1 mile further south but stayed on US 31, the main highway between South Bend and Indianapolis. Pete continued in the business, going to work every day, until the day of his death in December of 1999. His personal service was broken only by his four-year stint in the US Air Corps during World War II. During those years, his sales manager maintained and operated the business. By the 1990's, he had sold the business to his daughter but continued to actively entertain customers and follow up on service work as he had for more than 60 years. He was a dealer who stayed involved in both sides of the trailer coach industry as it split into two sides (housing and travel) in the 1950's. For his entire career he continued to sell homes and RV's on the same lot. When he began, there was little difference -- the owner determined if a unit would be a home or a travel trailers. Even after the size began to separate the units, Pete explained that, to him, it was very similar to an auto dealer selling both cars and trucks – they have different purposes but are sold very much alike.

Pete Callander's South Side Trailer Sales was easily recognized for years by all travelers between South Bend and Indianapolis. His long-time, highly visible, logo along US 31 was a huge 30-foot long replica of a pencil, poised at an angle, ready to write a deal, and proudly proclaiming him to be the industry's "Sharpest Pencil Man".

Pete Callander's contributions during his 60-plus-year career helped shape the industry, as well as build his iconic business. Never forgetting the early opposition to his trailer park, he spent his career in activities that generated public acceptance of the products he, and his competitors, sold. He was actively involved in local and national association leadership and in the development of retail shows. He was widely recognized not only for his years of enthusiastic support for the industry but for his tireless dedication to integrity as the basis for doing business.

For his lifetime of commitment to the industry he loved, Pete Callander was the very first dealer to be inducted into the RV/MH Hall of Fame as a member of the class of 1973. He continued to actively serve the industry for more than 25 more years after being nationally recognized for his already long career.

Chapter 9

Sheldon Coleman
The Growth Of Supplier R & D Departments

In 1925, a young engineer graduated from Cornell University, joined his father's company, and began a long career inventing and producing a wide variety of products and supplies to enhance the growth of the infant RV industry. As soon as kitchens began to appear in the early trailers and house cars of the 1920's, Coleman hot plates, stoves, lamps and lanterns were the RV appliance known to most campers. The Coleman Company was the first major supplier of these "creature comforts" to the early manufacturers. Sheldon Coleman spent more than 50 years developing and improving appliances and equipment to enhance the RV lifestyle. Among the first published aids to early RV'ers was the "Coleman Motor Campers Manual", a book of hints and "how to" articles published in 1926.

By 1936, the trailer coach industry was reported, in business surveys, to be the fastest growing industry in the country. The Coleman Company was racing to keep up with the dynamic industry's demand for heat, light, and cooking appliances.

In the early days of his career, Sheldon Coleman identified a weakness in the marketing structure of most industry suppliers. It was evident to him that there needed to be a much better engineering liaison between the manufacturer and his suppliers. In order to affect this liaison, he gave separate divisional status to his trailer coach industry business and assigned specialists in research and development, engineering, production, sales and service to become totally committed to improving his products and service to the industry.

Coleman strongly believed that his company needed to constantly expand and improve its products. Because of this, The Coleman Company was the first in the industry to establish its own research and development center. The early success of his engineering R & D center is illustrated by one of his "war stories". In June of 1942, he received a request from the U.S. Army Quartermaster for a one-man portable stove. The unit needed to operate on any available liquid fuel at temperatures from –60 to 125 degrees Fahrenheit and be no larger than a one-quart milk bottle. Reportedly, his first response was "it can't be done", followed quickly by "but we'll try". With assigned teams of engineers working around the clock, he successfully designed, prototyped, tested, got approval and began manufacturing and shipping the Coleman Pocket Stove. Five months after the Army's request, in November 1942, 5,000 units were in the hands of American GI's in the North African invasion. He later remarked that he was aware that common knowledge said that no successful product was ever designed by a committee. But in this case, his team concept worked.

Following the war, he observed that, in cold weather, while flies lived in paradise on the ceiling of most trailers, children froze on the floor. This led, in 1949, to the development of the down flow furnace, which blew warm air out at floor level and circulated heat throughout the trailers. The gravity heater, the most commonly used system of the time, heated the air at the ceiling level but could leave the floors extremely cold.

Coleman developed the technology that led to the manufacture of the first all-plastic insulated cooler. This was just one of the products popular among RV owners and outdoorsmen. In the 1960's, his products that were related to the RV industry grew to include tents, sleeping bags, catalytic heaters and folding tent-type camping trailers.

He was an avid proponent of customer service, guaranteeing the quality of his products. To follow up on this belief, he was among the first to establish a network of field service centers located throughout the country. This network eventually consisted of hundreds of authorized centers in 49 states and Canada with trained service personnel making on-the-spot Coleman service readily available to his customers.

The Coleman production facilities grew to keep up with the enormous growth in product variety and technology. In the 1960's, his plant in Wichita, Kansas, had grown to more than 1,000,000 square feet of production area. In one

An early ad for the Coleman Camping stove.

part of this facility, operators would feed a roll of steel, 67½ inches wide, into the assembly line. Through a succession of press operations, welders, and formers, a complete furnace casing unit that came off the end of the line every 34 seconds. After electrostatic painting and the addition of a grille, burner and controls, Coleman produced more than 1,000 furnaces for the RV and "mobile home" industry per day.

Sheldon strongly supported efforts to promote the industry. His company was typically one of the first suppliers to join state and national industry associations as they were formed. He personally took an active part in industry promotion events and was a ready participant in all regional and national trade shows, often manning his company's booth to interact with customers.

Upon joining his family's company immediately upon graduation from college, Sheldon Coleman quickly achieved notable recognition in the local community. Following a speech at Wichita State University in the mid 1930's, a student asked, "To what do you attribute your great success at such a young age?" to which he honestly replied, "Choosing the right father had a great deal to do with it." In spite of his having a head start in the industry, Sheldon was a tireless worker. He dedicated his entire life to making continual improvements and additions to The Coleman Company product line and its service to the RV, manufactured housing, and outdoor industry.

For his many contributions over more than 50 years of making the RV lifestyle more comfortable and enjoyable for all, Sheldon Coleman was inducted into the RV/MH Hall of Fame in the class of 1982.

Chapter 10

Robert Crist
Dealer Aftermarket Services

I n 1931, a Chicago auto dealer began to sell a few models of the new-fangled trailers on the lot beside his South Side Nash dealership. By 1933, the trailer venture had proved so successful that he became a dealer-distributor for several manufacturers. The car business had to move over to make way for the trailers. Robert Crist was quickly on his way to becoming the nation's largest trailer dealer of the 1930's. This was a case of history repeating  itself. Ten years before his venture into trailer sales, Crist had similar success in another sideline business when he became the nation's largest motorcycle distributor.

In 1936, he was operating his trailer business out of a 30,000 square-

foot, three story building on South Michigan Avenue in downtown Chicago. He used two floors to display his inventory and reserved the third floor for storage. His urban customers, who had no room on their small city lots to park their trailers, could rent space from him to store their trailers when not in use.

Within a few short years, The Robert Crist Company, having outgrown the three-story facility, moved one block north to a six-story building at 2309 South Michigan Avenue. This facility was actually two attached buildings. It gave Crist room to develop into what would be touted, in the late 1930's, as the "World's Largest Trailer Distributor". In the new facility, Crist had room set aside for an indoor display of his used trailer inventory. There were also rental storage spaces, a service department, and a sales area for trailer accessories - many of which he had invented or dramatically improved to make trailering easier for his customers.

He was recognized as the very first dealer to install aftermarket electric brakes on customer's trailers. Crist developed a device to automatically activate the brakes if the trailer separated from the tow vehicle. While he would install his brakes for local customers who could bring their trailer to his shop, Crist had an innovative approach to servicing out-of-state customers. His early national ads instructed trailer owners to "Just ship me your axle with hubs and bearings, leave them assembled. Do not send tires and wheels. I will return a complete outfit ready to bolt back on to your trailer springs together with a car control kit."

Among the accessories he developed was the Crist extension rear view mirror, which mounted to the hinge pin of the early car doors. It extended up to 18 inches to assist drivers in seeing around their trailers. He also developed the Crist puncture proof tubes for both trailer and car tires. Prices for the tubes ranged from $5.65 and $6.95, depending on tire size. The improvements on the Crist inner tubes gave earlier travelers considerable peace of mind. Before the puncture proof tire was available, travelers expected to have a flat tire every 500 to 1000 miles. He developed portable pressurized gas storage bottles and sold "Crist Gas" in twenty pound cylinders for the original butane trailer stoves. He also developed the Crist Trailer Shower, a gravity-fed appliance that held three and a quarter gallons of preheated water in an overhead tank. This gave the trailer owner the luxury of an on-board shower as opposed to having to go to the community shower house provided at early campgrounds. He created the Crist Metal Trunk, an all-steel weatherproof box that mounted on the rear bumper of a trailer to provide additional storage for the traveler.

Crist, recognizing the limits placed on his customers who needed to finance their purchases, started to provide his own financing. In the 1930's, the few banks that would finance the "gypsies and trailer trash" rigs, restricted the distance the owners could travel and the way they used the trailers. Finance companies also limited travel, to prevent owners from skipping out with their newly financed trailer. Crist's early ads in national magazines stated, "I do my own financing. You deal directly with me-not with a loan company. There is no restriction as to where you live or where you travel." His mid-1930's ads also offered rental trailers with option to purchase with total freedom to take the rental unit "anywhere".

The company eventually outgrew even the larger downtown facility and, in the 1950's, moved to 9300 Stoney Island where more land was available to display its growing inventory and the bigger units of the era.

Along the way, Crist found time to help organize and serve as a charter member of the Trailer Dealer's National Association (TDNA), the first national organization representing the dealers. This association, through

In the 1930's, the Crist Trailer Salon advertised its "Try It Before You Buy It" policy.

nearly seventy years of growth and reorganization, has become the RV Dealers Association (RVDA) of today. Crist served the association as vice president in 1954 and 1955, and held the office of president in 1956 and 1957. In 1975, the association recognized him with its first National Dealer of the Year Award in honor of his 45 years of contributions to the industry. In addition to his association work and duties as owner of the nation's largest dealership, he found time to write a monthly column of hints for RV owners. His column was published in Woodall's Trailer Travel magazine - the largest of the national RV consumer periodicals of the 1930's.

In the early 1960's, Robert Crist III began to take over the family operation from his father. In 1964, they opened a second dealership in Mesa, Arizona, at the request of Airstream Manufacturing whose products they sold. Airstream wanted a presence in the southwestern region of the United States. After moving part of the family's operation to Arizona, Robert Crist III began to develop RV parks. In the 1960, he developed Royal Glen RV Park in Glendale, the Aztec RV Resort in Mesa, and Orangewood Shadows RV resort. With the company's new interests in the southwest, it consolidated all of its operations in Arizona and, in 1972, closed its Chicago dealership.

Crist's many contributions to the RV world are considered modern and timely even today. He operated his business from an indoor showroom for both new and used models; he included a full parts and accessories retail center; he provided a fully equipped service department and installed the accessories he sold; he provided rental storage spaces for his customer's trailers; and he had rental unit availability.

Robert Crist died in 1975. His lifetime of contributions to the RV industry and its customers was honored with his posthumous induction into the RV/MH Hall of Fame in 1983.

The Robert Crist and Company dealership in Mesa, Arizona, is the direct continuation of the downtown Chicago operation founded by the first Robert in 1931. Run by Robert Crist IV, it is in the hands of the third generation of one of the RV world's founding families.

Chapter II

Kenneth W. Dixon
Pioneering Dealer Relations

In 1931, during the earliest days of the trailer coach industry, a southern California dreamer named Kenneth Dixon gathered up some parts from a wrecked 1928 Essex automobile, a few wooden 2 x 4's, some 2 x 2's and plywood, added some tarpaper, leatherette and canvas, and assembled his first travel trailer in a barn in the southwest section of Los Angeles. The chassis, other than the axle assembly and tow bar, was constructed of 2 x 4's. The framing for the body was made of 2 x 2's. The exterior was covered with leatherette except for the roof, which was canvas stretched over tarpaper. This prototype unit was complete with a small but functional back porch including a wrought iron guardrail and a canvas awning.

With no sales force or any association with trailer coach retailers, Dixon simply hung a hand painted for-sale sign on the trailer and parked it near the road in front of his small backyard barn-turn-factory. The first product sold quickly, and Dixon soon had an order for a second unit. With these two sales, Traveleze Industries was born. The fledgling company continued successfully, selling directly at the factory with no dealers or distributors, until 1936. At that time, Dixon began to cultivate and create a Traveleze dealer body. Many of the very early trailer manufacturers did not have franchise arrangements with specific dealers. Instead, they contracted with distributors to sell their products on a wholesale basis to any retailer wishing to purchase one or more units. Dixon was one of the very first manufacturers to create a franchise agreement, hoping it would build a loyal dealer following. After the first dealership was established in San Diego, the Traveleze dealer organization grew rapidly to than 100 franchisees serving the entire western half of the United States. In 1937, due in large part to orders generated through his dealer contacts, Dixon outgrew his original Los Angeles location. He moved his rapidly growing manufacturing operations to the San Fernando Valley community of Glendale.

In the later 1930's, Ken Dixon was recognized as an early industry activist

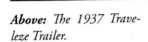

Above: *The 1937 Traveleze Trailer.*

Right: *A 1954 Traveleze Trailer.*

and promoter. He was one of the founders and ten charter members of the Los Angeles-based Trailer Coach Association (TCA), which represented trailer manufacturers in the western region of the United States. TCA, with its travel trailer division, was one of the precursors to today's RVIA. He continued his industry activism for many years, serving as a TCA board member through the 1950s.

As with most companies at the time, World War II brought Traveleze operations to a crawl. Manpower shortages and material rationing made production and distribution nearly impossible. However, by the end of the war, Traveleze had conceived and developed an assemble-it-yourself trailer kit in addition to their factory-assembled units. All components of the do-it yourself trailer were prefabricated and numbered. The proud new owner had the responsibility of assembling the pieces, by the numbers, upon delivery. Hundreds of these kits were sold through the late 1940's. Truckloads of the kits were shipped to Dixon's brother-in-law, John Bowater, in Minnesota. Bowater distributed the trailers, both in kit form and assembled, in the states east of the Mississippi River, giving Traveleze its first presence in that part of the county.

In 1947, ten years after their first relocation, and very shortly after the end of the war, Traveleze once again had to find larger quarters. This time, the company moved to Burbank, California. At this site, Traveleze developed products that would give the company its reputation for innovation. It was the first company to install a gas refrigerator in a trailer to replace the icebox that was the standard issue appliance at that time. In 1948, they created what was probably the first production chassis-mounted motorhome. They did this by mounting a trailer on the back of a pickup truck chassis. The chassis-mounted campers, popular through the 50's and early 60's, were the predecessors of today's type "C" motorhomes. In the post-war boom years, the company also developed a small but functional trailer. In a well-publicized promotional event, this trailer was pulled cross-country behind a motorcycle to demonstrate how light in weight and easy to tow it was.

Within only five years, the company outgrew the new Burbank plant and, in 1952, moved to a fourth location in Sun Valley, California. In the 1970's, as the industry met some of its most daunting economic challenges, three generations of the Dixon family were involved in the

Traveleze operations. Most of their dealers had a 20-years-relationship with the company that, in many cases, was as much friendship as it was business. With its dealers and family working together, the company successfully navigated the oil embargos and astronomical interest rates that destroyed nearly half of the RV industry in that decade.

The company continued as the industry's longest-lived family-held corporation until 1990 when it ceased operations. Thor Industries purchased and resurrected the Traveleze brand name as one of their RV brands in 1998.

Kenneth Dixon was a lifetime proponent of the RV lifestyle. He supported higher construction standards and sound engineering to promote safety in the industry. He was assuredly one of the visionaries who saw the great potential of self-contained travel for pleasure and business, and was a leader in the effort to build and promote quality and safety. Kenny was more than just a manufacturer, innovator, and industry leader. He was also an active consumer, spending a considerable portion of his leisure time, especially in his later years, RV'ing all over the United States in his Traveleze trailers. This helped him stay in direct contact with his consumers and let him get firsthand feedback from consumers and dealers.

For his pioneering efforts in the development of the RV industry, Kenneth W. Dixon was inducted into the RV/MH Hall of Fame as a member of the class of 1983. He passed away in December 1989 having served the industry, which he had helped to build, for nearly 60 years.

Chapter 12

Milo Miller

The School Teacher To An Industry

In the depression year of 1932, Milo Miller, an out-of-work painter and decorator from Mishawaka, Indiana, found himself on the road selling "Auto Top Rejuvenator". He had concocted this dressing from his own recipe of tar and gasoline to use on the coated canvas tops common on cars of the day. Milo missed his family and wanted them with him for at least part of the time he spent traveling. In order to join him on the road, his family had to have a place to live. So Milo designed a small "house trailer" to pull behind his Model A Ford.

He bought junk auto parts for an axle and frame and with a plywood floor and sides, built his first trailer in the back yard of his family home.

Miller began manufacturing the Sportsman trailer in 1932.

He built wooden frames to hold used auto glass for windows. Rubberized canvas, the same material used in auto roofs, was stretched over roof bows and down the sides to cover the plywood. Needing inexpensive adhesive to secure the covering, Milo used Karo syrup to fix the material to the wood. (He soon discovered that the sugar in the syrup attracted ants and bees. In subsequent models, he replaced the sugar with commercial adhesives.) With a coal-fired stove for heating and Coleman gasoline stove for cooking, the trailer was ready for travel.

Milo's practice on the road was to set up shop outside the gates of parking lots at large factories. He would sell the rejuvenator to workers as they arrived for work, then apply the dressing to their cars while they were at work. Their car, with the freshly rejuvenated top, was ready when they left for the day.

When school was out for his children, he and his family left on their first trip with the homemade house trailer. They made it as far as Midland, Michigan, where they set up housekeeping in the yard of a rural one-room schoolhouse. The family routinely used schoolyards as camping sites because a water well and an outhouse were always available. While at the Midland schoolyard, a passerby offered to buy his trailer at a price he could not refuse. Milo sold it on the spot. He went to a local junkyard and purchased parts for his second trailer, which he constructed in the schoolyard. This one also was sold before it ever left the schoolyard.

Recognizing the demand for his trailers, Milo Miller completed his planned sales trip, returned home and started the Sportsman Trailer Works. He produced a total of four trailers in 1932. In 1933, starting with an initial investment of $90, he created the Ideal Trailer Company. He began manufacturing his Sportsman brand trailers out of a rented shed in a Mishawaka lumberyard. The owner of the lumberyard advanced him materials on consignment: his credit was limited to one unit at a time. He continued to use junkyard auto axles but switched to oak timber for his frames. These first Sportsman trailers sold for only $168 each.

Later in 1934, he moved his rapidly growing operation ten miles east to a building on Harrison Street in Elkhart where larger, but still affordable, quarters were available. By 1936, his trailer manufacturing company had become very successful. In January he relocated again to yet larger quarters in the huge Noyes Carriage Works factory on the south side of Elkhart. Demand for his products continued to grow as did inter-

Miller's National Trailer Company provided military and defense plant housing during World War II, and grew to become one of the industry's giants of that era.

est in purchasing the company. In March, 1936, realizing a respectable profit, he sold Ideal Trailer Company to Wilbur Schult, who had been his national distributor and owned the local retail outlet. At this point, the company employed about 20 workers. The trailers now retailed for $300 - $500. After World War II, Ideal Trailer shifted its focus to the housing side of the industry and exists today as Schult Homes.

Miller immediately began another manufacturing operation in the basement space of the Noyes factory directly beneath the Sportsman/Schult operation. Just one month later, in April of 1936, Schult and his father purchased the building and asked Miller to move in order to make room for their planned expansion. Next, Miller rented space in the empty Elkhart railroad car repair facility and factory where, in the 1920's and early 1930's, the Elcar automobile had been built. Since ELCAR was prominently painted on the side of his building, he took that identity for his new product and began building Elcar Coach brand trailers. That company was quickly successful and in December of 1936, only nine months after it began operations, Miller sold Elcar Coach at a profit.

After creating two very successful trailer companies in Elkhart, Miller moved his base of operations to Huntington, Indiana. There, in 1937, he started the National Trailer Company. In mid 1939, he moved his entire operation to larger quarters in Elwood, Indiana. His workforce had mushroomed to 478 employees who produced 22 units per eight-hour day, in a factory with nearly 150 thousand square feet.

By 1938, trade magazine writers and editors were referring to Milo Miller as the "School Teacher" to the industry. This honorary title was applied not only because of the number of industry executives and owners who had begun their careers and learned their trade in one of his companies, but also because of often-copied assembly line technology that Miller developed. He was also the first trailer manufacturer to issue stock options as incentives for his employees.

At the beginning of World War II, the government needed trailers to use as temporary housing for military personnel and defense plant workers. This allowed some trailer builders to continue their operations when material rationing shut down others. His efforts in building house trailers for defense plant and military bases helped turn Miller's National Trailer Company into one of the country's giant manufacturers.

Milo Miller sold the National Trailer Company to his partner, Daniel Singer, and retired from manufacturing in 1945. In a career that lasted just over ten years during the earliest days of the RV industry, Milo Miller left a mark that few others could even imagine. For many years, he continued to guide the industry as a consultant to manufacturers who were trying to keep up with the growth in demand for trailer coaches. For his many contributions and amazing foresight, Milo Miller was inducted into the RV/MH Hall of Fame in 1975.

In response to his induction into the Hall of Fame, Milo wrote this personal history at 81 years of age:

Thank you so much for the honor bestowed
Upon a young man for the trailer he towed.
T'was in 1932 when it first began,
This great industry we are all in.

No factories being around,
I just started from the ground.
Back in '32 I built my first trailer
And by chance it was not a failure.

For what I say now is a fact,
The dumb thing sold just like that!
Of course it sold for just a song
For the great depression was still on.

Everyone said it would not last
My small business, which grew so fast
But those first years were rather bad
For few suppliers were to be had.

We made our own windows, doors and frames
Our moldings, hitches, and jacks the same.
The help from the auto factories was very real
For they supplied the axle, spring and wheel.

But to obtain them was really hard
For I rescued them from an old junkyard.
From the very start, my business grew
To 500 workers – quite a few.

In 1945 I decided to retire,
And no more workers did I hire.
Now I am retired with a grateful heart
Watching an industry grow I helped to start.

Now I am old and nothing wrong
Golf 18 holes and going strong
But I am looking forward to a better place
When I meet my maker face to face.

Chapter 13

Betty Orr
"First Lady" Of The RV Industry

In the late 1920s, Bertha M. "Betty" Orr and her husband operated a passenger bus line between Chicago, Illinois, and Davenport, Iowa. When she began to replace the older busses in their fleet, she noticed that many people were buying her obsolete motor coaches and converting them into the home-made "house car" motorhomes that were becoming popular at that time. In 1931, with the effects of the Great Depression wearing on her business, she sold the highway motor coach business and converted one of her own busses into a luxury "land yacht" for her own personal use. For much of the next year, she and her husband traveled the United States in their private house car. A few years later, seeing the many advantages to having detachable living quarters, she had the house car body removed from its bus chassis and converted into an aerocar style fifth wheel trailer, which she towed behind a coupe.

The Orrs fell in love with the trailer industry during their extensive travels. In 1933, they returned to Chicago and entered the business, opening Orr and Orr retail trailer sales, a franchise dealer for Silver Dome and Alma brand trailers. Orr's retail store, located at 2634 South Michigan Ave. in downtown Chicago, also carried an extensive line of repair and replacement parts and aftermarket accessories for the rapidly growing body of "trailerite" customers. When their business quickly outgrew its quarters on Michigan Avenue, the Orrs moved to a larger facility at 7334 Stoney Island.

In 1936, Orr became the interior designer and national sales Manager for Royal-Wilhelm Coach Company in Sturgis, Michigan, thus adding to her rapidly growing involvement in the trailer coach industry. Orr was more than likely the first female interior designer in the industry. With a woman's perspective, she made adjustments that made the trailers more livable. Her woman's touches, and the resulting improvements in livability, were well received by the growing body of serious and sometimes full-time trailerites. With this success, she moved on within a year to design interiors for trailers built by the Bender Body Company of Elyria, Ohio as well.

In 1937, Orr added to her lengthening list of industry firsts by designing and building what was perhaps the first custom commercial trailer towing rig. In her design, the bed of a Ford flatbed truck was extended and sloped so it could carry one trailer while towing a second unit. She used this rig to pick up and deliver units for her sales lot - thus avoiding factory delivery charges. Before Orr's towing rig, trailers were delivered one at a time, or picked up at the factory by the dealers who towed them behind personal vehicles.

In 1940, having gained extensive experience by designing and making innovations for other companies, she entered the manufacturing side of the industry. Orr began designing and building her own brand of custom Orr Trailers. These were widely recognized as high-end luxury travel trailers. She also began producing some very specialized commercial display units as well. Her commercial exhibit trailers were probably the first in the industry on which one complete side was removable for product display. Unfortunately, after less than two years of operation, World War II began, and with it, the strict material rationing which severely limited access to many products and components. This brought what had been a highly successful venture to a close.

Adding to her many credits, Orr designed and built the first fifth-wheel trailer and a customized truck to tow it. The earlier Curtiss Aerocar fifth-wheel trailers were all designed to tow behind an automobile. In 1955, after more than twenty years of operation, she closed her retail trailer sales operation to concentrate exclusively on her successful wholesale parts and supply business.

In addition to her many accomplishments as a businesswoman, Orr was extremely active on a local and national scale with industry organizations. She was a charter member of the Trailer Dealers National Association (later the Recreational Vehicle Dealers Association), and the first female member of its board of directors. She became the first female

Above: In 1937, Betty Orr designed and built a custom commercial trailer-towing rig that could carry one trailer while towing a second unit.

Right: An Orr Coach, built in 1940 at the Orr Trailer Company at 7916 S. Michigan Avenue, Chicago.

president of the TDNA in 1949 when she acted for Web Coulter, the elected president, during an illness that left him unable to complete his term. She was also the original chairman of the association's Manufacturer/Dealer Relations Committee.

On the local scene, Orr was elected Chairman of the Illinois Trailer Coach Association in 1951. With this, she became the first woman chairman of any state trailer industry association. As an active member of the national Mobile Home Manufacturers Association, she was the first female member of its Suppliers Board of Governors and was the first female member elected to the MHMA Board of Directors. She conceived the idea of an all industry forum for Mobile Home Manufacturers Association national show in 1955 at Cleveland, Ohio. Orr directed the forum, in which five panels of representatives from all segments of the industry made presentations and fielded questions from the members of the audience in attempt to increase the lines of communication between manufactures, suppliers and the retail dealers.

In the era when it was generally accepted that a woman's place was at home, Betty Orr made her mark as a dynamic and brilliant businesswoman. She had a national influence on the early development of the RV industry. Her influence was not derived from just observation and opinion, but from a deep, personal involvement in nearly every aspect of the growing industry. Because of her broad reaching industry involvement, she was a tireless proponent of cooperation and communication between the manufacturing and retail sides of the young industry. She retired from all industry activities in 1967 after more than thirty-five years of active national leadership and service and numerous successful business ventures.

In recognition of her many contributions as a retail dealer, inventor, manufacturer and supplier, and as a national association member and dynamic industry leader, Betty Orr was elected as a member of the very first class of inductees into the RV/MH Hall of Fame in 1972.

Chapter 14

Harold D. Platt
RV Man

In 1935, Harold Platt began his foray into the RV industry when he left his job as sales manager of a local gladiola farm, and joined his father Oliver and brother Eldon to purchase the Doloretta furniture company in Elkhart, Indiana. There, they began production of early house trailers. Oliver was a New York Central Railroad manager. The family also ran the St. Joseph Valley Silver-Black Fox Ranch, where they raised animals for the fur trade. Fur accessories and trim were popular at the time.

In the company's first year of operation, Mr. Rice, the man credited with inventing the waffle-style ice cream cone, asked the company to build a special trailer from which he could sell his popular

In 1935, Harold Platt began production of early "house trailers" at the site of the Doloretta Furniture Company in Elkhart, Indiana.

new product at carnivals and fairs. The trailer needed to have a large swing-up side window covered by an awning. This Platt-designed trailer, probably the first commercially built concession trailer, included a small living quarters in the front. Rice was so satisfied with his new trailer that he became a distributor for the company, demonstrating and selling Platt Concession Coaches at the events where he worked as a concessionaire.

Harold was a charter member and active in the creation of the Trailer Coach Manufacturers Association (TCMA). In 1937, he was on the committee to develop and promote the association's very first regional trailer show at the Tin Can Tourist Convention at Manistee, Michigan. With that beginning, he spent much of his long career developing, promoting and participating in both national and local trailer shows.

In 1937, Harold Platt built the first trailer to include a bathroom complete with tub. He was one of the first manufacturers to install a Coleman white gas kitchen range that included an oven in his trailers. This replaced the one or two burner countertop hot plate that had been commonly used up to that time.

When Oliver Platt died suddenly in 1939, Harold became president and CEO of the family business. Continuing as an industry activist, he was appointed by the national association to represent the fledgling trailer coach industry on the War Production Board during World War II. In this capacity, he helped coordinate the production and distribution of trailers for use as temporary living quarters at defense plants and military bases around the country. These defense contracts saved many manufacturers who would have otherwise gone out of business during World War II. Because of his demonstrated vision and leadership, he was elected President of TCMA in 1946, 1947, and 1948.

Following the war and through the 1950's, when most trailers were small, he built mobile homes under the brand "Platt Trail-a-Home". While they were identified as mobile homes, Harold explained that most of these early units were designed to be pulled behind the family car. As such, they were very much intended for travel and temporary use rather than full time living. Still some people chose to live in them full time.

In the 1950's, under government contract, he helped design and build several special, highly insulated units with skis rather than wheels. The U.S. Air Force used these in Greenland as part of the Cold War Early Warning System of radar

A late 1950s model Platt trailer.

bases. Some of these units were designed as dormitories: others were cooking and eating facilities. They were shipped to Greenland, and then slid over artic ice as they were pulled behind giant tractors to the large polar radar facilities.

In 1953, Platt was instrumental in developing the Midwest RV and Mobile Home show in Elkhart. By the late 1950's, that show was recognized as the nation's largest.

In 1960, 12-foot-wide mobile homes became popular, replacing the eight- and ten-foot -wide models available up to then. Platt closed his production plant, since the larger "12 wides" would not fit his assembly line and he did not wish to rebuild or relocate the factory. In 1962, at the age of 60, he became a retailer, opening Platt RV Sales on the north side of Elkhart near the new Interstate 80. In 1964, he became the first franchised dealer for the three Corson brothers. The Corsons were just starting RV production, calling themselves and their new company the Coachmen. Over the years, he became an early retailer and mentor for many of today's giant RV manufacturers. He was one of the very active founders of Recreational Vehicle Dealers Association (RDVA) and a life long advisor and counselor to dealers and manufacturers alike. For his exceedingly long career, Harold remained an active member and supporter of local, state, and national associations and shows to promote and benefit the industry he loved.

Because it seemed he could never get the RV industry out of his blood, Harold never truly retired from actively promoting its products. In 1996, at the age of 94, sixty years after he had assisted in the first national trailer show and at his own request, he manned a Coachmen Industries retail booth for three days at the Midwest Super Show at Notre Dame University in South Bend, Indiana. That show is the direct continuation of the Elkhart Show that he had helped to create 43 years earlier. *

Harold continued to actively serve as an officer of the local chapter of his state association well into the 1980's. By the time of his death in 1998, Harold had more elected positions and offices in more local, state, and national organizations and associations than any other individual in the industry's history.

For his life-long commitment and amazing contributions to the development, promotion, and growth of the trailer industry as a manufacturer, retailer, and association leader, Harold D. Platt was inducted into the RV/MH Hall of Fame in 1975.

*The author had the fortunate opportunity to interview Harold at that show. It was apparent that, while somewhat frail with age, he was mentally sharp and still had the same enthusiasm for his beloved industry as his fellow salesmen, some of whom were 70 years his junior.

Chapter 15

John A. Schroeder
The "Dean of the Trailer Industry"

In 1898, John A. Schroeder, a young Swedish engineer, immigrated to the United States. He quickly became a major influence in the birth of the American automobile industry, first as chief engineer at Standard Roller Bearing Company and later, vice president of sales and engineering for the Elgin Motorcar Company. He later became general manger of Wills-St. Claire, Inc., an early auto manufacturer. During his rise in the auto industry, he was attracted, to another industry in its infancy, travel trailers. Schroeder first experience with trailers was as a consumer: he built his first trailer in 1922 for his own use. Soon Schroeder was an enthusiastic promoter of the industry, even though it was not generally well received by Americans, who identified it with gypsies and ne'er-do-wells.

In 1928, Schroeder left the automobile industry to become principal owner of The Detroit Aerocar Company, one of the early fifth-wheel trailer manufacturing companies. The Aerocar was built using designs licensed by Glenn Curtiss, inventor of the fifth-wheel hitch and owner of the Curtiss Aerocar Company in Jacksonville, Florida. These two were among the first companies in the nation to manufacture solely recreational vehicles.

Seven years later, in 1935, Schroeder sold his interest in Detroit Aerocar, left trailer manufacturing behind, and entered the component supplier side of the now exploding industry. He became the head of sales for the trailer division of the Liggett Spring and Axle Company (predecessor to today's S.H. Liggett Co.). In this position, he became one of the first outspoken proponents of industry standards for quality and safety. As an engineer, he was very specific in his recommendations.

By 1937, his positions were so widely known and so well accepted that the early trade magazines began to call him the "dean" of the trailer industry. Later that year, he convinced the C. H. Warner Company to develop electrically activated trailer brakes. These replaced the earlier hydraulic brakes, that were similar to automobile brakes, but had a history of poor performance in early trailers. In fact, Schroeder had installed

A Detroit Aerocar made in the 1930s by Schroeder's company. This is a modern photo of a unit that has been restored and owned by Ken Hindley of Union, Ontario.

hydraulic brakes on the trailer he built in 1922 and, was therefore personally familiar with their complexity and lack of reliability. The early hydraulic systems required multiple master cylinders and had a complicated linkage to the brake system on the tow vehicle. Warner's electric brakes were much simpler and more reliable. They quickly became factory options as well as a common dealer-installed aftermarket addition to existing trailers.

Schroeder is also credited with convincing the Budd Company to develop and distribute a stronger wheel that was specially engineered for use in trailers. In his sales contacts with trailer manufacturers all across the country, he represented not only his own company, but also all manufacturers who built the safer undercarriage components he engineered. In this regard, John Schroeder was very probably the original manufacturer's representative in the RV industry.

He believed that the old practice where manufacturers produced their own components from in-house design was a recipe for disaster. Schroeder was vigorous in his belief that trailer components should be engineered, developed, and manufactured by knowledgeable specialists.

In the mid 1930's, Schroeder was one of the original charter members of the Trailer Coach Manufacturers Association (TCMA), the first predecessor of today's Recreational Vehicle Industry Association (RVIA). In his work with this association, he was a staunch advocate of safety and quality standards. In this, he led the fight to have the association regulate the early trailer camps for cleanliness, sanitation facilities (most early trailers had no toilet or sanitary facilities), and unit spacing. He campaigned actively for measures that would assure consumer safety and comfort. In his opinion, this was the best way to turn around the public's opinion of the industry.

In 1938, Schroeder was involved in the birth of the short-lived American Travel Trailer Association. Cornelius Vanderbilt Jr., the son of the shipping and railroad magnate Commodore Vanderbilt, led the ATTA. Cornelius Vanderbilt was an internationally recognized writer who lived in a trailer while traveling. The association was an attempt to combine the interests of manufacturers, suppliers, dealers and distributors, park owners, and consumers into a single voice. The ATTA board of directors included committees and representatives from each of these interest groups. Schroeder was appointed the original chairman of the group's engineering and standards committee. In a nationally published article in December 1938, he wrote, "This industry will not meet its potential without actively supporting good products, good roads, good trailer camps and service facilities throughout this country."

That same year, he wrote about his acquisition of Detroit Aerocar ten years earlier. "After studying it from all angles, I determined that there was a great future for trailer coaches and that a new industry was making its debut. For several years many of my friends took great delight in kidding me about fooling away my time and money. They were thoroughly convinced that people would not drive on the roads with "that thing" dangling about back there. It has become a matter of pride with me to prove them wrong".

When John A. Schroeder died, in December of 1947, he was the only individual who had been an honorary lifetime member of the TCMA. Schroeder played a key role in the growth of the American auto industry as well as in RV manufacturing and in the development of a dynamic supplier function. His insistence on safety and quality became the cornerstone on which the industry grew into the giant that it is today.

Chapter 16

Wilbur Schult
Industry Leadership Through Acquisition

I n the summer of 1933, Wilbur Schult, a young, Elkhart, Indiana clothing store clerk visited the Chicago World's Fair. At the fair, he fell in love with the new-fangled travel trailers that he saw there. One evening after he returned home, he was in downtown Elkhart enjoying an ice cream cone with his parents and was amazed when a car drove by with one of the trailers in tow. He brashly asked the owner if he could see the unit. The trailer was one of Arthur Sherman's Covered Wagon. When he realized the company was located in a suburb north of Detroit, Schult was determined to not only get one of his own, but to become a dealer as well. With the Depression still in full swing, capital for investing in such a venture was nearly impossible to obtain. Schult tried to borrow startup money from his father. But his father refused to support him, calling the idea a crazy folly. He eventually borrowed $300 in "pin money" from his more sympathetic mother. With his mother's money in hand, he made the trip to Mt. Clemons, Michigan to get his first trailer. He bought his original unit for $275 and towed it back to Elkhart behind his own car. He set up his retail operation, with one unit in inventory, on the street in front of his parent's clothing store.

After several weeks, he made his first sale and his dream was underway. Unfortunately, the check that he had accepted for the unit bounced, leaving him with only $25 of his mother's loan left—and no inventory. With the naïve faith of youth, he returned to Mt. Clemons to try to get a second unit on consignment. Amazingly, he got that second unit, and towed it back home to start again. This time he had better luck. The trailer sold quickly, and the check written to pay for it cleared the bank. His business was off and running. Shortly after his first sale, he added Milo Miller's Sportsman trailers, made in Mishawaka, Indiana, to his dealership.

With enthusiasm fuelled by his belief in the industry, his business enjoyed rapid success. He sold a total of 138 units the first year and, in late 1934, signed a contract to be the national distributor for Sportsman, a new but growing brand of trailer. Sportsman had moved its operation from a shed in Mishawaka to a small facility the size of a three-car garage in Elkhart. By this time the burgeoning Schult retail sales business had moved from its original street-front location to a large lot on the city's near eastside. Schult's business quickly became national in scope. He advertised monthly in both Billboard and Variety magazines to attract vaudeville and carnival clientele. In January of 1936, Sportsman trailers moved again to accommodate its growing production, this time into one of the largest buildings in Elkhart. In March of 1936, when Milo Miller sold his manufacturing concern to his national distributor, the Schult Trailer Company was added to the Schult Trailer Mart.

With this expansion, Wilbur Schult began to make his mark on the new industry. He went through a period of explosive growth, fueled by acquisition that was unequalled in the industry's history. He discontinued his retail agreement with Covered Wagon, which at that time was

1937 Nomad

the largest company in the industry. Next, he began to rapidly recruit dealers for his own brand. By April, 1937, Schult had two plants in Elkhart with more than 250,000 combined square-feet of manufacturing space. He had an additional division in Ottawa, Ontario, Canada. He acquired the Pathfinder Trailer facility in Elkhart. With this acquisition, he had the largest production capacity of any company in the industry. In 1937, he produced more than 1500 trailers. He continued his dramatic growth by acquiring the Royal Wilhelm Company, the manufacturers of Royal Coach from Sturgis, Michigan. He opened a division in Christchurch, New Zealand, which probably made him among — if not the first manufacturer producing on two continents, in three countries. He also developed a licensed distributor agency in Sweden.

Beginning in 1938, Schult's father William was designated a roving ambassador. The elder Schult was now the corporate secretary-treasurer of the company he called a folly only 18 months earlier. As the ambassador, he represented the Schult Trailer Company at all TCT and ATA events, rallies, and major festivals.

By the start of 1939, Schult Trailers, Inc. had supplanted Covered Wagon as the largest company in the industry. Wilbur Schult was very active in the newly formed Trailer Coach Manufacturers Association (the early predecessor to RVIA) and was elected its national chairman in 1940. A firm believer in promotional events, he was the National Trailer Show Director, a position he held for 14 years.

As he dramatically increased the industry's production capacity, he also earned a reputation for design innovations. Schult was the first

1930's ad for Schult Trailer factory in Elkhart, Indiana.

manufacturer to extend standard width from seven-and-one-half to a full eight feet as well as the first to offer seven-and-one-half-foot ceilings. He was the first manufacturer to build a full steel frame under his entry level products. He designed and installed an optional full trailer air conditioning system that circulated air over a vault of ice to cool the trailer. In 1938, he built a luxurious custom 40-foot fifth-wheel rig for New England publisher Myron Zobel that included a customized towing vehicle. Dubbed the "Continental Clipper", it included a stainless steel kitchen, a radio-telephone, and a flying bridge where the Zobels could ride behind the chauffeur-driven tow vehicle. This unit earned so much notoriety that Zobel sold it to King Farouk of Egypt after personally using it for seven years.

Schult was the first RV manufacturer to prove that a great company could be built both through direct growth and through acquisition. This model is still used by industry leaders seventy years later.

Schult's business maintained its dramatic growth through WWII by completely converting its operation to defense production. He built specialty trailers to transport the huge paratrooper gliders from point to point, and converted Ford sedans into wooden bodied military ambulances. He built busses to that had a variety of use during the war including personnel and POW transport. The special "dead transport" busses were designed to respectfully carry the bodies of soldiers killed in battle to the rear lincs. His Elkhart operation alone kept more than 600 people employed around-the-clock during the war.

In the 1950's, the industry evolved into two separate segments, recreational vehicles and mobile homes. Deciding to pursue the housing segment, the Schult Trailer Company was renamed the Schult Mobile Home Company. Schult sold his interest in the company in 1957, but continued to serve the industry through association work and other ventures. The company continues today as Schult Homes, the oldest company in the housing industry.

For his many contributions to the growth and development of the entire industry, Wilbur Schult was inducted into the RV/MH Hall of Fame as a member of its original class in 1972.

Arthur G. Sherman
The "Father Of The RV Industry"

I n the summer of 1928, the president of a Detroit pharmaceutical company decided to take his family camping and fishing in northern Michigan. For the trip, he purchased one of the new-fangled tent-trailers. It was really a tent in a wheeled box that had to be assembled upon arrival at the campsite. There was little resemblance to today's folding tent trailers. The instruction booklet and advertising described in glowing terms how this fantastic device could easily be set up in ten minutes or less. Arthur Sherman and his family arrived at their fishing site after dark, in the midst of a heavy downpour of rain. With illustrated instructions in hand, and his wife and five children waiting in the car, Sherman set out in the rain to erect their new shelter for the very first time. One hour later, when he still had not succeeded, the family came out to assist their now-drenched father. They eventually succeeded, but Sherman's faith in the products of the infant camping vehicle industry was destroyed. He was not, however, deterred from his desire to enjoy the benefits of auto camping.

After his vacation, Sherman decided he could design and build a camping trailer that did not have to be assembled at the campsite. Over the winter, he built a functional trailer, and the next summer returned to northern Michigan to try again. His first camping trailer was nine feet long by six feet wide and about five feet high at the center. It had a rear entry door with a center aisle that could be dropped down behind the axle to allow for more headroom. The top half was canvas stretched over curved bows in the style of a Conestoga wagon. His unit was very functional and an instant hit with his neighbors at the campsite. He built his camping trailer with no intentions of turning it into a second career. But, if the response to his homemade unit was any indication, he recognized a sizable demand for such a simple camping trailer. Sherman was neither an engineer nor a manufacturer, but a self-sufficient scientist who was fairly handy with building tools.

Following this much more satisfactory trip, Sherman began to fur-

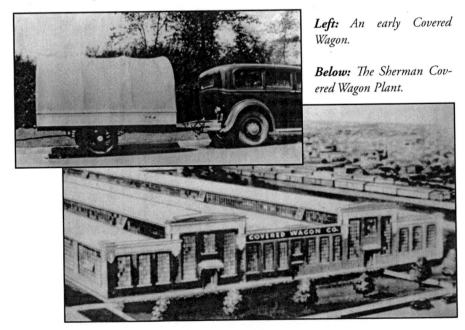

Left: *An early Covered Wagon.*

Below: *The Sherman Covered Wagon Plant.*

ther investigate the potential demand for his unique little trailer. He hired a couple of local carpenters to help build a few units to display at the Detroit auto show in the fall of 1929. His units were an instant success. At his introductory exhibit, he sold all of his show models, and took orders for another 117 units. All of this happened while the trailer was still a concept, before he had a production facility. He quickly hired 20 employees and began building the "covered wagons", the name his children had given to the their camping trailer. This original trailer was six feet wide, nine foot long and five feet high, with a rear entry door. In order to provide headroom for the cook and other occupants, Sherman designed the floor behind the axle to drop to the ground. When down, canvas sides protected the floor and created additional standing space.

The Covered Wagon Company grew so rapidly that within a couple of years it had to relocate from the original Detroit facility to a much larger plant in nearby Mt. Clemens. By 1935, Sherman was producing 35 units per day. Customers could choose from a wide variety of models with state-of-the-art features. By 1936, production exceeded 50 units per day from a single plant. In addition to trailer assembly, the plant had a mill to cut all of lumber used in production, a cabinet shop, and a furniture shop to produce all of the cushions and mattresses. In 1936, Sherman's company was by far the nation's largest in the rapidly growing industry, producing about one out of six of the trailers made in America. In 1937, Fortune magazine heralded Arthur Sherman as "the Henry Ford of the trailer industry".

Sherman, an avid yachtsman, was the owner and captain of a 90-foot yacht, the "Meredon", as well as the Fleet Captain of the Detroit Yacht Club. With this background, many of the appointments in his early trailer designs had a distinctive yachting influence. The mahogany interiors in his deluxe models, the positioning of overhead cove cabinetry throughout the unit rather just in the galley, cutty storage compartments under beds and benches, and roof vents that simulated nautical hatches were all features that could be traced to his yachting experience.

Early on, he recognized that many of the technological advances being developed Detroit automotive manufacturers could be adapted to trailer production. Sherman picked the brains of auto industry friends and acquaintances for plant design ideas. He was the first to build his trailers on a massive scale using an assembly line similar to that used in automobile production He developed "Sherman Steel", a process where plywood paneling was laminated to light gauge steel. This was a radical change from the technology used in earlier trailer production, where units were typically covered with a skin of Masonite, homosote, or plywood protected by a layer of leatherette. The leatherette covers were applied with inexpensive adhesives—even, in one case, Karo syrup.

In 1936, Sherman became the first manufacturer to offer his dealers inventory financing. He developed a program through C.I.T. Financial Corporation where dealers could acquire an inventory of trailers with only a 10% deposit. They would pay 1.5% on a 90-day-floor plan on the remaining balance. This was huge advance in dealer relations and one of the primary reasons Sherman held such a large share of the market.

Unfortunately, the rapid and dynamic growth of The Covered Wagon Company was also its downfall. In 1938, in an attempt to increase production to 100 units per day, Sherman contracted with the Motor Wheel Corporation for wheel and axle assemblies. But two events followed that impacted the trailer market. A slight economic recession slowed demand for the product. But equally important was the trend toward a wider unit. Other manufacturers had increased trailer width to eight feet. Demand for the wider units grew . Soon orders for Covered Wagons tricked to 10 or 15 per day. The expense of reworking a huge stock of axle assemblies, and the imminence of World War II ended the reign of Covered Wagon as the industry giant in 1939. The company ceased all civilian production in 1941. It made some units under government contract during the War but never resumed production after the war.

In 1974, Arthur Sherman was recognized for his many contributions to the early development of the trailer coach industry with induction into the RV/MH Hall of Fame. Today's RV manufacturers and dealers alike can thank him for his forethought in bringing mass production, the marine influence to interior design and inventory financing for dealers to the industry.

Industry Builders

Want A Good Buy On A Used RV?

Did you ever wonder who built the very first motorhome? We don't know if this "cave-man" was the first, but it certainly could be.

Walter T. Drawe, Jr., a sales representatives for United Sales of Texas, figured he would like to share a bit of our industry's history. Walt's dad used this 1927 Model T Ford chassis "motorhome" to travel to the river on weekends. His favorite camping haven was 12 miles away from his home and he very rarely missed the opportunity to drive his "home-on-wheels" to the campsite.

I wonder if Mr. Drawe, Sr. ever looked into the future to get a feeling for what his seedling would grow into. I often try to imagine what RVs will look like 50 years from now.

Thank you, Mr. Drawe, for sharing your memory from the past with all of us. —CS

Chapter 18

Wally Byam
King Of The Caravans

As the Airstream Company, founded in 1932, resumed trailer production following its shut down by the material shortages of World War II, Wally Byam turned the day-to-day operation of his company over to others. This left him free to develop an idea he has been harboring, caravan RV travel. As everyone who knew him would attest, Wally was never satisfied with the basic or mundane. Point-to-point in the good ole' USA was just not good enough in his great scheme of life. He had enjoyed many challenging adventures pulling his own unit and was sure that others would enjoy group RV travel. From the early 1950's through the mid 1960's, he conceived, planned, organized and led large groups of trailer tourists on 27 exotic trips. The destinations included Mexico, Central and South America, Canada, Alaska, Europe, Africa, China...even around the world. All caravan units were trailers pulled by a car or truck. No motorized units participated in any of his caravans. The early caravans were open to all brands of trailers. Later, only Airstream owners were invited on the caravans. Wally realized early in his caravan career was that RV'ers who visited foreign lands were not there to create good will on behalf of the United States. They were simply tourists, out to enjoy the sights, sounds, and differences in the people and places they visited. Members of the caravans tried to be good citizens and respected the laws and traditions of the country in which they were guests. In many cases, the political climate of their host country made it mandatory that the travelers be very wary of what they said and how they behaved.

In some ways, Wally utilized the same skills to plan the caravans that he did to build his business. With pilot trips, advance arrangements, and political expediency, his international trips ran smoothly. For his 1951 trip, the caravan left from El Paso, Texas, and traveled through Mexico, Guatemala, El Salvador, Honduras, Nicaragua, and Costa Rica to the Panama Canal. He led 63 RV units on a round trip journey that required passports, visas, food drops, gas drops, medical arrangements and all manner of special details that were unnecessary in domestic RV travel. This trip is generally thought to be the very first international RV caravan. He found that towropes and winches were absolutely essential in many areas. Roads and bridges were sometime figments of some mapmaker's imagination! The 25 or so exotic RV adventures that followed over the next 15 years, although quite expensive, were very popular. In 1955 and 1956, after almost six years of organizing trips through North and Central America, he planned a trip through Europe. The caravan visited Italy, the French Riviera, Spain, then went north through all of Western Europe to Sweden and Norway. On this trip he learned that trans Atlantic shipping companies would not transport more than twelve car-trailer units on a given ship. The bulk space in a ship's hold that was taken up by a car or truck with a trailer did not equal the ballast weight required for that amount of cargo space. Because of this, the 35 units on this first overseas caravan were relegated to three different ships and arrival schedules. The group departure date had to be delayed until all participants arrived. On this trip, at least, travel was entirely on improved and mapped roads through towns with available services. Some trips were not so easy.

The African caravan from Capetown, South Africa to Cairo, Egypt, took more than two years to arrange. The terrain was so difficult that each of the forty-one trailers had to be pulled by a four-wheel-drive truck. The caravan left Capetown on June 30, 1959, and arrived at Cairo 221 days later on February 19, 1960. Along the 14,307 miles, they broke their own trails and forded streams where there were no bridges. Occasionally, road scouts were sent ahead to see if any civil wars had broken out, that would negate any prior travel arrangements made during the pilot trip. Travelers in this caravan ranged from six to eighty-five years of age. The oldest member was a physician, who provided medical care to his fellow travelers. The trailers varied in length from sixteen feet to thirty feet: the average was twenty-two feet in length. On his subsequent trips through Africa and the later on the 1964-65 "Caravan Around the World", arrangements had to be made with oil companies and trucking firms to send fuel, oil and mechanical supplies to meet the caravan at points en route when there were hundreds of miles between commercial fueling station.

Wally Byam passed away in 1962 but his team of exotic caravan developers carried on with his dreams. As if the challenges of a south

The Around the World caravan stopped at the Greek ruins.

to north trip through Africa had not been enough, in 1964 they left the Philippine Islands to fulfill one of Wally's dreams. Following closely to the historic caravan route mapped out by Marco Polo in 1273, the caravan traveled west through China, Cambodia, Thailand, India, Pakistan, Afghanistan, Iran, Iraq, Syria, Turkey and on into Greece, and Italy. Then it was back through France and north again to Scandinavia. Promoted as the Wally Byam Around-the-World Caravan, it was documented in a series of TV shows supported by the National Geographic Society and narrated by movie star Vincent Price. These shows were the catalyst for an explosion in the popularity of RV's in the late 1960's.

On his caravans and through his other travels, Wally espoused his Four Freedoms of RV travel:

- **Freedom from arrangements**-reservations, schedules, taxis and tips. "You do not have to worry about your reservations in the next town or where you are going to sleep tonight. You have all of your accommodations right there with you. Home is where you stop."
- **Freedom from the problems of age**-"For some, checkers, clubs, gardening and grandchildren are not enough. Out of this boredom, ailments are born."
- **Freedom to know**-"You meet people on a plane or a train and the next day you separate. When you travel in a trailer, you meet people in their homes and they meet you in yours."
- **Freedom for fun**-"To relax and lose yourself mentally."

Wally Byam's well publicized adventures around the world expanded RV owners' imagination. But they also introduced the RV to parts of the world where automobiles were rarely seen, much less one pulling a house behind it. As the adventures gained worldwide fame and acceptance, it was easier to travel, even through the most remote countries.

Wally Byam's success in building the concept of caravan travel added yet another feature to the wonderful world of self-contained travel. For his many contributions to RV's and the RV lifestyle, Wally Byam was posthumously elected as a member of the first class inducted into the RV/MH Hall of Fame in 1972.

Chapter 19

John C. Crean
Industry Genius

T o coin a phrase from the George M. Cohen song, John C. Crean was a real Yankee Doodle Dandy. Born on the Fourth of July in 1925, his relationship with RV's began when he was just four years old. In 1929, his father packed the family into a homemade house car built on an old truck chassis to travel from the family's dirt farm in North Dakota to California in search of work.

At 17, young Crean lied about his age and joined the US Navy during World War II. After he was injured and discharged from the Navy, Crean turned around and joined the Merchant Marine to continue his service to his country.

Immediately after the war John joined the Blackhawk Company, a

An early Fleetwood trailer

California manufacturer of house trailers. He started his career in the RV industry earning ninety cents an hour. But he was a quick study with a compulsive work ethic and a knack for motivating people. With these skills, he soon learned all he could about the trailer industry. In just six months, he was the general manager of the plant, at a salary of $175 a week.

In 1947, he joined the larger Viking Trailer Company. At Viking, he could be involved in all aspects of production, from design to construction. Under his valuable leadership and input, Viking grew and became a nationally recognized manufacturer.

In 1950, John invented and patented a new style of Venetian blinds for trailers. A year later, when Viking chose not to produce and install his invention in its units, he and his wife, Donna, formed the Coach Specialties Company. They built and sold blinds to many southern California coach builders. Even with his own specialties company, Crean missed being involved in trailer production. He was soon designing and building trailers again. When the trailer sales grew, he changed the new company name to Fleetwood Enterprises, after the popular luxury automobile.

In the mid 1950's, following the Korean War, the trailer industry was having a difficult time. In planning his survival strategy, John established a set of personal policies to which he would adhere in his business. They were: 1) sell only for cash--extend no credit; 2) assess personnel on performance not on personality; 3) recognize employee and dealer loyalty; 4) recognize demand and greatest sales potential; and 5), the one tenant that he later violated with regularity, do not get involved with industry politics or associations.

The company grew into a national giant and was at one time the nation's largest producer of both manufactured homes and recreational vehicles. Although he was not personally involved, Cream instructed his top company executives to, "Get involved in industry activities when you are needed and where you are needed". That early corporate directive, in total violation of his early tenants, resulted in Fleetwood Enterprises having a presence on associations across the country. A member of the Fleetwood Enterprises management team has, at one time, served as chairman of every national trade organization. Fleetwood's managers have been equally represented on the board of directors of state and regional associations across the country.

In 1965, John Crean took his 15-year-old company public. Its first public financial statement showed $18.5 million in annual sales. Just eight years later, his financial statement showed $350 million in sales and a workforce of more than 7,000 employees. Four years later, after the country had weathered the oil embargo and astronomical interest rates of the 1970's had killed or crippled other manufacturers in the industry, Fleetwood reported $565 million in sales and more than 9000 employees.

Crean never wanted to be tied to his desk in the chairman's suite. Throughout his entire career, it was as common to see him in overalls on the assembly line or in the prototype shop helping to develop new products as it was to spot him in a suit in the executive suite.

During most of his career, Crean and his wife, Donna, took an annual trip, touring the United States in one of his motor homes. During the six or eight weeks of travel, the couple stayed at public campgrounds. Traveling in this manner let him get a first-hand feel for consumers' needs and changing interests. One time he commented that if he heard the same feature discussed at four different locations around the country, it was a sure sign of a trend. He would take the problems back to his company to resolve, and the ideas would go into research and development.

In spite of his hands-on style of management, John Crean had many other interests outside of directing the continued growth of his company. His down-to-earth style prevailed in all parts of his life. Never being the type for a showy mansion in the city, Crean made his home on a ranch in the California desert near San Juan Capistrano. A lifelong supporter of organizations serving youth, he made the open land portion of his "Rancho Capistrano" available to youth groups such as the Boy Scouts, Girl Scouts, church groups, YMCA, YWCA and others to use at no cost for outdoor recreational activities. Years later, the entire 96-acre ranch was donated to Evangelist Dr. Robert Schuller as the site for his world renowned "Crystal Cathedral".

Crean had an avid interest in auto racing, both as an owner and a driver. With actor James Garner, he co-sponsored a racing team based at the Ontario, California race track. At one time, he and wife Donna held the Husband-Wife class record for the grueling off-road race between Tijuana and LaPaz, Baja California. Not satisfied with just land-based activities, Crean expanded his activities to the sea. He designed and built his own 76-foot-long ocean cruising yacht on which he spent many days sailing on the Pacific Ocean.

While still chairman and CEO of Fleetwood, Crean took another of his hobbies public. Based on his personal knowledge of gourmet cooking, he developed and starred in a gourmet cooking show that aired on cable television in southern California. The show was popular with a wide audience, and was eventually featured every Wednesday morning as part of ABC television's "Home Show".

In 1998, at the age of 73, John Crean retired from Fleetwood Enterprises. He divested himself of his interest in the company to follow his many other interests full time. For his many inventions and contributions to the growth and development of the RV world, John C. Crean was inducted into the RV/MH Hall of Fame as a member of the class of 1985. John C. Crean passed away on January 11, 2007.

--------- *Chapter 20* ---------

Don Boles
A Dedication To Quality

I n 1939, Don Boles, an enthusiastic young southern Californian, was one of thirty-seven
candidates chosen to take part in a
four-year tool and die maker apprenticeship. His was in the first class of
program administered by the U.S.
Department of Labor in a plan designed by President Franklin Roo-
sevelt to help the country recover
from the Great Depression. Boles
was assigned to work and study at the
Lockheed Aircraft Company plant in
Burbank, California. There he learned all aspects of aircraft design and
construction as well as how to build tools and component parts. While
in the program, he earned a number of awards for tools he designed and
built that improved on methods used to fabricate aluminum parts.

After graduating from the apprenticeship program in 1943, he worked briefly for General Electric Company in Cleveland, Ohio. When World War II began, he enlisted in the Navy. Following boot camp, he was stationed at a military base in Norman, Oklahoma. With a wife and three children and no available housing, Boles purchased a 27-foot trailer. This was home during his entire stint in the Navy.

After VJ Day and his release from the Navy, Boles hooked up his trailer and used the trip back to California as a family vacation. When they arrived back home in California, he parked the trailer in his driveway with a "For Sale" sign on it. That very day, he sold the trailer, at a profit, to the first people who stopped to look. Even after it sold, several people stopped by to try to buy the trailer. With this response, Boles recognized the there was pent-up, post-war demand for good trailers. Even as he went back to work as a civilian, he began to design a trailer. With his aircraft training, his design included top quality features, including lightweight, all-riveted all-aluminum construction. With financial help and moral support from his father, he began to build his first trailer. While he and his father looked for vacant factory space, his construction plant was his single car garage. The trailer length was limited to nine and one-half feet, the length of a garage. Fortunately, he and his father soon found an available and affordable site and began construction of their trailer factory.

When a friend of Don's became interested in the venture, the two formed a partnership. They called the company B and R Manufacturing and dubbed the trailers they built "Roadrunners". They finished the first unit while still operating out of the garage. As before, they parked the trailer, with a "For Sale" attached. This time the trailer was parked on the street in front the site for their soon-to-be-built factory, next to the mason's supply of sand and bricks. Once again, the first customer to look at it purchased the trailer for the asking price of $675. The father of one of their neighbors was so impressed with the design and quality of the new products that he placed an order for ten trailers to use in his business. However, he needed twelve-foot-long units. With the limitations in size of Boles' garage, the partners had to wait until their factory opened to begin work on this order.

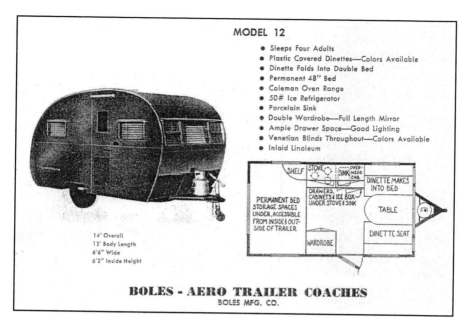

MODEL 12

- Sleeps Four Adults
- Plastic Covered Dinettes—Colors Available
- Dinette Folds Into Double Bed
- Permanent 48" Bed
- Coleman Oven Range
- 50# Ice Refrigerator
- Porcelain Sink
- Double Wardrobe—Full Length Mirror
- Ample Drawer Space—Good Lighting
- Venetian Blinds Throughout—Colors Available
- Inlaid Linoleum

SHELF STOVE OVER-HEAD CAB. DINETTE MAKES INTO BED

PERMANENT BED STORAGE SPACES UNDER, ACCESSIBLE FROM INSIDE & OUT-SIDE OF TRAILER

DRAWERS, CABINETS & ICE BOX UNDER STOVE & SINK

SINK

TABLE

DINETTE SEAT

WARDROBE

14' Overall
12' Body Length
6'6" Wide
6'2" Inside Height

BOLES - AERO TRAILER COACHES
BOLES MFG. CO.

The stress of ownership increased during the factory construction and related financial problems. Because of this, Boles' partner pulled out of the business agreement. Don took full control of the company, changing the name to Boles Manufacturing. Later, he renamed the trailer the Boles Aero. When the trailers proved popular with consumers, production increased. The company's early problems soon faded. In 1946, the company's first year in business, Boles Manufacturing had shipped more than 300 trailers from its new factory. The continuing success of his trailer business made it possible for Don to quit his outside job. He no longer needed that income for security for his family. Production of various models of the Boles Aero high-line travel trailers continued for more than thirty years until the company permanently closed its doors in 1980. By this time, the company was building units that were 27 to 35 feet long, which was the new standard in the travel trailer market. The modern units had comfortable appointments.

In the 1950's, Boles was active in promoting the industry as well as his new company. He was instrumental in founding the consumer rally and show that, by the mid 1960's, became the Dodger Stadium trailer show. For many years, this was the world's largest RV event.

Among his contributions to RV design over the years are the flush vent covers for water heaters and furnaces, recessed fillers for water tanks, and recessed door handles. All of this gave the trailer a smooth exterior line. Even though he introduced these design elements in the early 1960's, many of his innovations, in an upgraded form, are still in use today. Boles worked with a German manufacturer of small diesel chassis to produce a small front wheel drive diesel "type C" motorhome in the late 1960's. He developed this motorhome at the same time that truck chassis-mounted units were beginning to become popular.

During the Vietnam War, Boles Aero designed and built mobile photo labs. These were shipped by giant cargo aircraft to the Far East for use by the US Air Force in developing aerial surveillance camera film. They were also used as mobile medical and dental clinics to provide service to civilians in developing communities.

Don Boles was an active member of the Los Angeles-based Trailer Coach Association, (TCA), serving on its board of directors for more than 30 years. He was instrumental in the creation of a separate division of TCA for travel trailer manufacturers. For most of his career, he was active in the TCA and in the Chicago-based Mobile Home Manufacturers Association. He was also a charter member of the American Institute of Travel Trailers, the first association created specifically for RV manufacturers and the predecessor of today's RVIA. Boles' success was proof that a well-designed, high-quality travel trailer could be sold successfully, even as many manufacturers were cutting costs and prices to become more competitive.

From his earliest involvement, Don Boles was a strong proponent of strict industry standards for safety and quality. He was instrumental in the lengthy and very political undertaking of getting one set of national standards approved and enforced industry-wide.

For his many contributions to the RV industry over his lengthy career, Don Boles was elected to the RV/MH Hall of Fame as a member of the class of 2005.

Chapter 21

Ray Frank
Father Of The Motorhome

In 1958, Ray Frank owned a small trailer manufacturing company in Brown City, Michigan, a small town north of Detroit, on Michigan's east coast. Frank designed and built a small house car solely for his personal use. The name house car had been given to self-propelled RV's when the first one was built in the early 1900's. But the Frank family called their RV a motorhome. The coach was unique in that it was designed from the ground up to be a motorized recreation vehicle. It was neither a trailer to which additional wheels and an engine were added, nor converted from a bus or truck chassis. By changing its name, Frank unwittingly began a transition from the house cars that existed 40 years earlier to modern motorized recreational vehicles.

This first motorhome was popular with campers the Frank family met in their travels. Because of the interest that other RV'ers showed, and with little success in finding components for his own unit, Ray approached the Dodge Division of Chrysler Corporation with a request to purchase a bulk quantity of bare truck chassis on which he could produce more of his coaches. Dodge refused to sell its chassis to him directly, instead referring him to a nearby Dodge truck dealer. Frank negotiated a contract with the dealer, Lloyd Bridges, to purchase 100 chassis. When Bridges signed on as Frank's first dealer, the first motorized RV dealership and the beginning of Frank's franchise organization was created. That original dealership is still in operation today under the management of Bridges' sons.

Frank started production of his line of motorhomes as a sideline to his trailer business. He built six units in 1960 and 131 in 1961. With that growth in production, the name was changed from Frank Motorhomes to Dodge Motorhomes. These units were the first motorhomes produced on an assembly line. For its first three years in production, Frank's motorhomes were designed around a box-like aluminum body and featured the industry's first molded fiberglass nose and tail section. In 1963, a rounded, all-fiberglass body was introduced, using a design and renderings created by Ray's 18-year-old son Ron. Even at that age, Ron's eye for style and design was obvious. During these years, demand accelerated rapidly: production increased to more than 700 units per year. The new all fiberglass-bodied Dodge Motorhomes, available in 21 and 27-foot models, took the RV industry by storm. The Dodge Motorhomes were sold through car and truck dealers as well as RV dealers, which gave Frank more sales outlets and contributed in part to his rapid success. The motorhomes were also considerably more affordable than the custom units available through other manufacturers.

There were a number of innovative features in the Dodge Motorhome. The couch could be converted into a double bunk bed when the back was suspended from the ceiling by heavy straps to form the upper bunk. Models included a double-basin stainless-steel sink, and draperies that enclosed the windshield for privacy. When demand for the relatively inexpensive motorhome continued to grow rapidly, other manufacturers began producing similar models. Still, from 1966 to 1967, more Dodge motorhomes were registered on the road in the United States than all other brands of motorized RV's combined.

In 1967, Frank Motorhome Corporation was sold to PRF Industries and became the Travco Division of PRF. From this date on, the coaches were identified as Travco motorhomes or as Dodge-Travco motorhomes. In 1979, Travco Division was sold by PRF and became a part of Clarence Fore's Foretravel, Inc. Coincidentally, Foretravel, Inc. had grown from a single coach that was privately made and intended for personal use, just as Frank's company had.

After he sold Dodge Motorhomes, Frank continued to bring innovation and improvements to the RV industry. He felt that many American consumers wanted a smaller, more compact motorhome that would be easier to drive, easier to park, and comparatively easier to buy. To fulfill what he perceived as a need in the market, Frank developed the Xplorer brand of van-based motorhomes. Production of the first Frank Industries "van campers" began in 1968 with a fully self-contained model that would fit in any standard-sized residential single car garage. Frank once again caught

This Xplorer was the first Type B motorhome built in the United States.

industry attention with the first production "Type B" motorhome. Until his model, the only similar unit was built in Germany using the underpowered Volkswagen microbus.

With his success in the design and production of the first motorhome as a totally original vehicle from the ground up, Frank paved the way for the development of the "type A" motorhome industry. With his motorhome, Frank established a new style of RV travel that thrives today. His production of van-based mini motorhomes led to the successful development of yet another segment of the RV industry. When his innovations in interior appointments are added to his development of the Type A and Type B motorhomes, it is clear that Ray Frank has earned the title of "Father of the Motorhome".

For his many invaluable contributions to the creation and growth of the modern motorhome industry, Ray Frank was inducted into the RV/MH Hall of Fame as a member of the class of 1978.

Chapter 22

John K. Hanson
A Motorhome For Everyman

I n 1957, John K. Hanson, a businessman in Forest City, Iowa, was elected to chair that community's development commission. As owner of the local furniture store, the combined Oldsmobile automotive and International Harvester farm implement dealerships and the local funeral home, he was the obvious choice to spearhead the effort to attract business to the town. The commission set out to recruit an RV manufacturer after learning about that industry's amazing growth. Members of the commission convinced Modernistic Industries, which produced the Aljo brand of trailer, to relocate its plant from California to Forest City. The plant originally employed 17 people.

Before the move was complete, a strike and adverse financial conditions in California caused the parent company to fail. With the investment made by local stockholders at risk, five businessmen from Forest City purchased the outstanding stock. When the new company was founded, Forest City, Iowa had less than 3,000 citizens.

In 1958, Hanson was 45 years old, and a successful local funeral director - furniture dealer - car and tractor dealer - who had just added RV dealer to his resume when he signed a franchise deal with Mallard travel trailers. But when asked, he accepted the offer to act as president of Modernistic Industries. He accepted the position with the understanding that he would serve in that position for just one year to help the community get this new venture underway. Shortly after Hanson took over the reins of the company, its name was changed to Winnebago Industries in recognition of the historic Native American tribe after whom the county was named.

Hanson earned local and national recognition as an innovator and salesman. In the late 1940's, he was featured in Time Magazine for his store's well-publicized policy of bartering furniture for farm goods with the local farmers. In his system, a rocking chair cost a dozen bushels of grain and a refrigerator cost three hogs. With this system, he could have grain to feed the livestock until he could liquidate his inventory.

In his other business ventures, Hanson had been active in the related industry associa-

The Winnebago motorhome was introduced in 1966.

tions. He continued that practice in his presidency at Winnebago. In 1959, with no local or state association representing the RV industry in Iowa, he joined the Indiana Mobile Home Association. Hanson wanted his company to be responsible and provide its customers with a safe product. He was concerned that the industry was developing a bad reputation because of the many poorly constructed trailers that were on the market. Because of his reputation as an advocate of quality and safety, Hanson was guest member of the Mobile Home Manufacturers Association's (MHMA) committee to develop industry standards even before Winnebago Industries was a corporate member.

In 1960, three years into his one-year term, he formed the Stitchcraft Division to produce all the cushions and draperies used in Winnebago recreational vehicles. This gave the company better control over quality and costs. Then, on September 24, 1964, disaster struck. The entire

Winnebago production facility burned to the ground in an early morning fire that destroyed the entire inventory of parts, jigs, fixtures, and plans. Before the smoke cleared, Hanson went to work to rebuild the plant. By noon that day, he had met with the SBA and local bankers to arrange financing on a new facility. They broke ground on October 17, twenty-three days after the fire. Production resumed five months later.

In the mid-1960's, Hanson developed sandwich panel technology. In this, the aluminum skin for an RV's exterior walls is bonded to the insulation and interior paneling. He believed that the sandwich panels were stronger and safer. So strong was his belief that he incorporated sandwich panes into the design of the original Winnebago motorhomes. To prove his point he sent the panels to the Alcoa aluminum technical center to be tested for long-term durability. A man of great integrity, Hanson refused to promote his product without confirmation. His conviction was so strong that he refused to unveil his new Winnebago motorhome at the 1966 national RV show in Louisville, Kentucky until the test results came in from Alcoa. When he got the report by telephone at the show, he unveiled the new Winnebago and a new era in RV history began.

The original Winnebago motorhome was mass-produced on an assembly line. The first model sold for less than $5,000. At this price, it opened up the motorhome market to working class families. The brand became so popular that by the 1970's, Winnebago was the generic term for the RV industry, much like Kleenex and Frigidaire were for their respective industries. That original class A motorhome was produced in three model sizes, 17, 19, and 22 feet long. Even though they were innovative for the time, they were a far cry from the units that are popular today. Each slept six on three available double beds. The bathroom, with shower, was only 30-inches square.

In the mid 1970s, John K., as he was known, was 65 and ready to retire to a retreat in Hawaii. About the same time, oil shortages and high interest rates had ruined many leading RV manufacturers. Winnebago's future was also in doubt. By 1979, not willing to stand and watch his company fail and his friends and neighbors loose their livelihoods, John K. came out of retirement to reassume leadership of the company. He continued to actively lead the company until the mid-1990's when he was well into his eighties.

In 1976, at the national RV show in Louisville, Winnebago introduced the Winnebago Heli-Home, a helicopter-based flying RV. This model was intended to make travel to out-of-the-way destinations available. When travelers arrived at their destination, the helicopter would convert to a comfortable living space. Although this model was innovative, it was not a success.

By 1969, two years after the Winnebago motorhome was introduced, the company employed 1,252 employees, a considerable increase over the original 17 with which it started operations. Today Winnebago employs 3,500 people in four northern-Iowa facilities. The company's hometown has an official population of only 4,200. Some employees are bussed to work daily from as far as 50 miles away.

A current model of the Winnebago motorhome. (Courtesy of Winnebago Industries, Inc.)

During his career in the RV industry, John K. Hanson served on the boards of directors of MHMA, the Recreational Vehicle Institute, (RVI) and the Recreational Vehicle Industry Association (RVIA). As chairman of its board of governors, Hanson assisted in the merger of the RV division of MHMA with the RVI. In addition to his leadership in national associations, Hanson was active in numerous state and regional associations.

A genius in business who was dedicated to technological innovation and strict quality standards, Hanson changed the face of the RV industry. He proved that an affordable, quality RV could be mass-produced and made available to thousands of Americans. When John K. passed to his reward on 1996, his one-year commitment to the citizens of Forest City, Iowa, had stretched into a world-changing career of more than 35 years.

For his commitment to industry standards and quality and his many contributions to the development of affordable motorhomes, John K. Hanson was inducted into the RV/MH Hall of Fame in 1983. This was one of many honors bestowed on him in commemoration of his lifetime of accomplishments. In 1984, he was recognized by the King of Norway as a successful son of Norway. In 1986, he received the RVIA Distinguished Service to the RV Industry Award. And in 1994, he was recognized by the RV Dealers Association as a Titan of the industry.

Chapter 23

Eugene Vesely
The Development Of Tent Campers

In the mid 1950's, Gene Vesely, a Lapeer, Michigan, construction worker was planning a long-anticipated camping vacation with his wife. However, Mrs. Vesely decided that she really did not want to sleep in a tent on the ground. So she asked him to find a solution to their sleeping problems. Given the task of saving his vacation and keeping his wife happy, Vesely designed a simple wooden platform that could set on an old boat trailer frame. Although this got them off of the ground, it was not a not a satisfactory solution. When he went back to his drawing board, he came up with a box trailer, about the size of a double bed, out of which a tent could be unfolded. The trailer bed, which held a mattress as a liner, made a comfortable

An early Apache tent trailer.

sleeping area. The trailer was small and easy to pull. The sitting and cooking area of the tent actually stood on the ground beside the trailer-bed. Thus the Apache camping trailer was born. After gauging the interest shown in his trailer by his fellow campers during his family trips, Vesely determined that there was in fact a demand for the light, simple, tent camper trailer.

The concept of a towable tent trailer was far from new. The first camping trailers were built at the turn of the century. But many of the very early tent campers were designed to be pulled with the canvas already erected over rigid iron pipe frames. The earliest autos traveled at speeds of 15 to 20 miles per hour. At this speed, there was no problem in transporting the already erect tent campers. Up until Vesely's foldout design, most trailers of the period held the tent for storage and transportation, but had to be totally assembled and set up upon arrival at the campsite. His concept of a fold-up tent trailer was unique, especially one with the living area standing off the side of the trailer box.

Vesely had only an eighth-grade education but was adept at design. He was an astute businessman who understood that the camping consumer wanted equipment that was serviceable and a good value. Vesely had timing on his side. The baby boomer generation's growing interest in camping and outdoor recreation created a surge of demand for his easy-to-use, easy-to-tow tent trailer. Vesely began production of the Apache brand trailer in his hometown in the thumb region of upper Michigan.

By 1957 he had moved his operation to a new, larger manufacturing plant. By 1961, he had a second plant in operation in Lapeer and soon after opened a third factory in Elkhart, Indiana. By this time, the 600 workers employed at the Apache Trailer Company were building 2,000 campers a month. In the 1960's, camping trailers were so popular that they were sold through RV dealers across the county, as well as by mail

An Apache solid-state camping trailer.

order through such catalog giants as Sears & Roebuck and Montgomery Ward. Seeing the opportunity to widen his customer base, Vesely built trailers that were sold under those store brand names, in addition to his Apache brand.

In 1970, Vesely introduced a solid state folding camping trailer that eliminated canvas sides on folding camper trailers. Apache released a unit with a hard plastic roof and modular rigid side panels that were inserted into place after the roof was raised into position. The first year, these units had solid panels in the trailer body itself but canvas sides on the tip out beds. In the 1971 models, canvas was totally eliminated. Some models of the solid state Apache trailers folded out on all sides to sleep up to eight occupants. This unique unit paved the way for many of today's collapsible solid-state units.

As the company grew, other innovative features were available on the Apache models. These included fold-up tent units with on-board toilet facilities, hot water showers, a range hood over the stove, and a unit with an outside accessible "basement" storage compartment for luggage or additional supplies. Vesely Manufacturing also built conventional travel trailers and even a class C type motorhome. Still, the true Apache claim to fame is the wide variety of models and innovations available on its tent trailers.

Eugene Vesely sold his company to outside investors in 1980. This was the beginning of the end of the Apache trailer. The new owners shut down Vesely Manufacturing, selling off all of the company's assets, including the Apache brand name. Another manufacturing company, unrelated to the RV industry, now uses the Apache brand. By this time, Eugene Vesely had gone on to another career. True to his reputation, he was as successful in his new venture as he had been in his trailer manufacturing business. In his new venture as a breeder and raiser of world class show cattle, he traveled to exhibitions in all corners of the world.

The tent camper had been around for fifty years when Eugene Vesely designed his travel trailer. But it was his innovations and marketing genius that dramatically changed the tent trailer industry. His products remain so popular today that various companies throughout the nation still provide replacement parts including full canvas kits made from the original factory plans. Even though the manufacture of this brand of travel trailer has long ceased, the Apache trailer and its reputation live on. The fact that folding camper trailers continue to hold a significant share in the RV market is a tribute to the inventions of an eighth-grade dropout.

For his many contributions to the RV lifestyle and his ingenuity in developing many variations of the folding camping trailer, Eugene Vesely was honored with induction into the RV/MH Hall of Fame in the class of 1976.

Chapter 24

Merle D. McNamee
King Of The Kampers

In the early 1950s, Merle D. Mc-Namee, an avid camper, outdoorsman and Boy Scout leader, wanted to expand on the ways he could use his pickup truck in these ventures. McNamee was not alone in his devotion to his truck. The pickup truck's popularity had grown since World War II, particularly with those who were familiar with the WWII multi-purpose vehicle. A sheet metal contractor by trade, the enterprising Californian designed and produced the first slide in camping units that had features for cargo and campers. His first prototype units were simple cargo shells with cots or mattresses that would be thrown in for sleeping after the equipment was removed at the campsite. Hunters and campers responded enthusiastically to the prototypes.

As a result, in 1952 McNamee formed Kamp King Coaches. He began to develop a variety of camper products for pick up trucks that he produced at his Rosemead, California plant. With rapid growth of his venture, he outgrew his first location and had to move to a new facility in El Monte, California by 1957. Through the early years, he pioneered many truck camper features still in common use today. These include stand up ceiling height, cab-over design, all riveted aluminum construction, and boxed in compartments on 10 foot models with the overhang lowered below bumper height. He also designed built in jacks for easy unit installation and removal. These replaced the contractor's scaffold jacks that were originally carried for the purpose. The molded fiberglass tops he designed eliminated seam leaks. The units with a sky rider design had seats in the cab-over section. Kamp King Coaches was one of the first manufacturers to outfit campers with built-in cabinets for storage as well as complete deluxe appliances including refrigerators, kitchen ranges, hot water showers, and toilets.

By the late 1950's, hybrid models were available with suspended foldout canvas bedrooms. McNamee began building models with all molded fiberglass shells in 1958, long before most RV manufacturers had begun to accept fiberglass as a building material. In the 1960s, he

An early slide-in camper.

The cab over camper had expanded sleeping room.

designed and built a special unit that sat on the top and over the back of the early four-wheel-drive sports utility vehicles, such as the Ford Bronco, International Harvester Scout, and Chevy Blazer. Given the name, "Custom Hi-Country Camper, these units included a full-length cab-over section and could be used on or off of the vehicle. However, they had only limited success because of the unwieldy weight on top of the vehicle.

In the late 1950s, in order to reduce the weight on his larger campers, he began building units with sandwich foam panels with wood panel interior and aluminum exterior. These panels proved to be much stronger and lighter than the conventional sidewall construction in use at the time. He built and sold these sandwich panels to other camper manufacturers even after Kamp King stopped producing campers in 1969.

McNamee actively lobbied truck manufacturers to develop the three-quarter ton "camper special" vehicles that would insure that trucks had the ability to safely carry campers. Many new owners, trying to use their campers on half ton vehicles, were traveling severely overloaded. Some of these early units weighed 2500 to 3000 pounds dry weight. Provisions and supplies added even more weight. Owners were trying to drive a vehicle loaded with almost twice the load for which it was designed. This created a life-threatening safety hazard for campers, which tainted the industry's reputation. McNamee was successful in his efforts with truck manufacturers who were supplying trucks with the larger payload by the late 1960's.

As his units became longer, larger, and heavier, he pioneered the process of removing the original truck cargo bed and building chassis-mounted campers. These eventually morphed into today's type "C" motorhomes. On some of these larger models, McNamee designed roof top patios and fold-up additional sleeping space in second story rooms. He was also the first to design a unit by converting early vans. In this, he chopped off the body of the van behind the driving area and integrating the campers on the chassis.

He built specialty units for celebrities, including Roy Rogers and "The Lone Ranger" Clayton Moore. The publicity generated by a star's use of these units generated a broader interest in this type of camper. The early truck campers were used primarily by hunters and fisherman, and not considered acceptable to most family campers. Celebrity endorsements changed that.

McNamee was instrumental in the founding and development of the Portable Camp Coach Association for manufacturers of slide-in campers. Early in its history, he served as president and sat on its board of directors for most of the years the association was in existence. In 1965, through PCCA, he was instrumental in the passage of the excise tax cut bill through the U.S. Senate. This bill removed federal excise tax from articles designed to be placed on trucks or on truck chassis. This bill relieved motorhome owners from the tax as well.

McNamee was widely recognized for his ingenuity, his political acumen and the advances he made in customer relations. He ran his business on the theory that "customers must come first". His commitment to customer satisfaction was well known even by the industry press. There are many reports of "Mac" personally performing minor repairs on units brought to the factory for warranty problems. He would even stop to fix a camper at a rally or public gather, assuring that his customer was satisfied before he went back to the event. He remained an avid camper, using his outdoor activities as an opportunity to field test his products. He came back from his outings with ideas for changes and improvements.

Merle McNamee's success in developing slide-in truck campers for pickup trucks was a remarkable display of his ingenuity. His success is even more astounding considering that he built it on a product that had yet to achieve public acceptance. The pickup of the 1950's had yet to develop the popularity or features that are seen in the modern-day vehicle. His contribution in the development of the chassis mounted camper and its evolution into the modern type C rigs is yet another of McNamee's contributions to the RV industry and its consumers.

For his many accomplishments in the development of truck campers and his lasting impression on the RV industry in general, Merle D. McNamee was inducted into the RV/MH Hall of Fame as a member of the class of 1992.

Chapter 25

HERB REEVES, JR.

"He just couldn't hold a job!"

While Herbert M. Reeves, Jr. was still in the U.S. Army at the end of World War II, he bought a small travel trailer to use for camping. After a few trips, he fell madly in love with the travel trailer lifestyle. When he was discharged from the service in 1946, he returned home to Kankakee, Illinois, and opened Reeves Trailer Sales. He wanted to give his friends and neighbors the chance to enjoy the outdoors and the freedom of the RV experience.

His retail business was successful, and grew quickly. But, like many before him, he felt the wanderlust that strikes many in the industry. The need to travel was much like that felt by our country's early pioneers.

Covered Wagon Trailer

He sold the sales lot, left Kankakee, and moved his family to the trailer production center of Elkhart, Indiana. There, he started up the Florence Stove Distributing Company and began the wholesale distribution of the new "bottled gas" ranges. These were rapidly replacing the white gas ranges that had been the industry standard since the early 1930s. Through the fifties, bottled butane and propane gas had become the fuels of choice in cook stoves, heaters, wall-mounted lights and even refrigerators in both travel trailers and mobile homes. As a result, every manufacturer needed a source for gas appliances. As with his trailer sales, this venture enjoyed early success and quickly grew. Through this business, Herb became acquainted with many of the successful manufacturers of that era.

In 1958, Reeves changed horses. After a visit to the Arthur Sherman family at their retirement home in northern Michigan, he acquired the rights and logos to the storied brand name. In the 1930's, the Shermans had been the largest trailer manufacturer in the industry. Their Covered Wagon trailer was the first of the industry's national giants. With these rights and company identity in hand, Reeves reestablished the Covered Wagon brand name and became a travel trailer manufacturer. Herb owned and operated the second generation Covered Wagon Trailer Company in Elkhart from 1958 until 1965. During this time, he achieved several industry firsts, including the development of space inside the rear bumper to store the flexible sewer lines used to dump the on-board waste tanks. He designed a rear-access built-in storage trunk. Reeves developed a technique to build three totally diverse units (trailer, fifth-wheel, and slide-in truck camper) simultaneously in the same plant.

In 1965, he changed directions again when he sold the Covered Wagon manufacturing company, and opened the Arrowhead Park Campground in southern Michigan. As a campground owner, he entered his fourth segment of the RV industry. Although Arrowhead Park was a successful venture in its own right, Reeves was not as successful in developing a national franchise of the campground.

While involved in each of his brief, but successful, RV careers, Reeves supported the industry through his involvement in associations. In the fifties, he was a faculty member of the Trailer Dealers Association national service schools, which served dealer technicians across the nation. He became a member of the board of governors of the Indiana Mobile Home Association travel trailer division and served as the director of that association's first RV show. He was a member of the board of governors of the TCMA/MHMA (Trailer Coach Manufacturers Association – later the Mobile Home Manufacturers Association) travel trailer division. He also served on the board of the Mobile Home Craftsman's Guild, which was responsible, in large part, for the move towards uniform industry standards. He even served a short stint as the interim Executive Director of the guild.

In the 1960's, he was elected to the board of directors of the rebel, and short-lived, American Institute of Travel Trailer and Camper Manufacturers. This association was an early attempt to create an organization for RV manufacturers that was totally separate from the mobile home associations of which they had historically been a part. Later, he chaired the committee that formed the more successful Recreational Vehicle Institute (RVI), which later evolved into the RVIA (Recreational Vehicle Industry Association) of today.

After becoming a campground operator, Reeves still had the urge to actively serve in an association. Finding no local organization for campground operators to join, he became chairman of the committee that founded the Michigan Association of Private Campground Operators (MAPCO). He served as the group's original executive director from 1970 until 1976 while still operating his successful campground. As ex-

ecutive director, he developed a comprehensive statewide campground and RV service directory. This highly touted directory was distributed to consumers, setting a pattern for the directories and guides used by many RV enthusiasts today.

With his widely varied but influential career now more than 30 years old, Herb Reeves was recognized for his years of dedicated service to the growth of the industry by induction into the RV/MH Hall of Fame in the class of 1979. In his response to being honored by his peers at the Hall of Fame induction ceremony, Reeves wrote, "I don't know why you would want to honor this guy, he's just a job hopper, he can't even hold a job."

This nationally recognized honor provided Reeves with yet another opportunity to serve the industry he loved. In 1981, by invitation, he became the Executive Vice President of the RV/MH Hall of Fame Foundation, a position he held until 1989, when the office for the foundation was relocated from Reeves home office to its first permanent home. While serving the RV/MH Hall of Fame Foundation, his fifth career in the industry, Herb traveled around the country attending shows and exhibitions, maintaining his contact with the huge variety of friends that he had developed throughout the industry.

With his penchant for organizational involvement and leadership, Herb Reeves, Jr., played a key role in the growth and development of nearly every aspect of the RV industry.

About The Author
Al Hesselbart

A former police officer, not-for-profit executive, teacher, and salesman, Al Hesselbart has had a widely varied career.

A native of Michigan and graduate of Michigan State University, he was an officer with the Michigan State University Department of Public Safety for 5 years And also served on the faculty of the Mid-Michigan Police Academy. Following that, he turned to the not-for-profit sector, joining the Boy Scouts of America as a national field worker. He led summer camps and outdoor activities for more than fifteen years. In the 1980s, he enjoyed great success in automobile sales at an import car dealership in Elkhart, Indiana.

Hesselbart's next professional foray would draw on his knowledge of automobiles, his success in the not-for-profit sector and his knowledge of the outdoors. In 1994, Carl A. Ehry, president of the RV/MH Heritage Foundation asked Hesselbart to become the general manager for the organization. Somewhere in his tenure with the organization, the duties of historian were added to his responsibilities.

When Hesselbart began with the organization, its offices were located in a 20,000-square-foot warehouse/office complex on Benham Ave. in Elkhart. At that time, the Foundation had just begun to its collection of historical artifacts. Hesselbart gradually increased its holdings, adding slide and photographic collections from industry enthusiasts, and completing the collection of historical periodicals. Along the way, Al Hesselbart became one of the foremost authorities on the history of the Recreational Vehicle and Manufactured Housing industries. He has written articles for national magazines and newspapers and been quoted as an authority in the New York Times, U.S.A. Today, Reuters news service and the Associated Press. He has appeared in documentaries on both industries that have appeared on the Travel Channel, Home and Garden Channel, CMT, PBS, and Canada's HistoryTV and at large RV rallies and events around the country.

The RV/MH Heritage Foundation was formed on March 22, 1972 by a group of trade and consumer magazine publishers attending the Mobile Home Manufacturers' Association (MHMA) meeting in Washington D.C. In its original charter, the Foundation, then named the RV/MH Hall of Fame Foundation, was given the responsibility for restoring and perpetuating the history of the two important industries it represented. In addition to creating a hall of fame to honor key individuals, the Foundation was to be a repository for documents, publications, photos, and displays significant to the history of the recreational vehicle and mobile home industries. This archives developed into the most significant collection of historical data available relating to the two industries.

Between 1990 and March 2007, the Foundation housed the archives with their offices in a 20,000-square-foot complex in downtown Elkhart, Indiana. With major gifts from Winnebago Industries, Thor Industries and Champion Enterprises and additional gifts from many industry companies and individuals along with major support from the RVIA "Go RVing" Campaign, the Foundation raised $6.5 million to build a new facility. An endowment gift from Roger and Waneta Reynolds helps assure operational funding. Ground was broken for the new project on August 2, 2005. Located at exit 96 of the I 80-90 Toll Road, the RV/MH Hall of Fame opened its doors to the public on March 26, 2007.

The 50,000 square foot facility includes a 5,000 square foot archival library, a 5,000 square foot exhibit hall, a 85 seat theater, a 5,000 square foot Go RVing -World of Tomorrow exhibit, and more than 20,000 square feet to display historic units of the RV and manufactured housing industries.

An important gallery in the new facility displays the members of the Foundation's Hall of Fame. Each year, since its founding in 1972, the Heritage Foundation has honored those industry leaders who made an exceptional contribution with induction into the Hall of Fame. Photos of more than 200 of these leaders grace the central gallery of the new Museum.

The museum is open to the public from 9 AM to 5 PM Monday through Saturday. Admission is $8 general, $6 for seniors and $3 for youth 6-16.

For more information on the museum, contact Al Hesselbart, general manager and historian, at 574-293-2344, or by email at rvmhhall@aol.com. You can see the museum on the internet www.rvmhheritage-foundation.org

CPSIA information can be obtained
at www.ICGtesting.com
Printed in the USA
FFOW04n0942090815
15770FF